PUNK ROCK

BY SIMON STEPHENS

DRAMATISTS
PLAY SERVICE
INC.

The New York premiere of PUNK ROCK was produced by MCC Theater (Robert LuPone, Bernard Telsey, William Cantler, Artistic Directors; Blake West, Executive Director) on October 29, 2014. It was directed by Trip Cullman. The scenic design was by Mark Wendland; the costume design was by Clint Ramos; the lighting design was by Japhy Weideman; the sound design was by Darron L West; and the dialect coach was Stephen Gabis. The cast was as follows:

WILLIAM CARLISLE	Douglas Smith
LILLY CAHILL	Colby Minifie
BENNETT FRANCIS	Will Pullen
CISSY FRANKS	Lilly Englert
NICHOLAS CHATMAN	Pico Alexander
TANYA GLEASON	Annie Funke
CHADWICK MEADE	Noah Robbins
DR. RICHARD HARVEY	David Greenspan

CHARACTERS

WILLIAM CARLISLE

LILLY CAHILL

BENNETT FRANCIS

CISSY FRANKS

NICHOLAS CHATMAN

TANYA GLEASON

CHADWICK MEADE

DR. RICHARD HARVEY

PLACE

The first six scenes of the play are set in the library of the Sixth Form of a fee-paying grammar school in Stockport.

The seventh scene is set in Suttons Manor Hospital.

TIME

The play is set in the present day.

NOTE ON SONGS

All songs indicated in the opening scene stage directions are themes for each scene, not songs to be played aloud. If you would like to play the specific songs in your production, you must clear performance rights with the respective copyright holders. For more information, please see the Special Note on Songs and Recordings on the copyright page of this acting edition.

PUNK ROCK

ACT ONE

Scene 1

"Kerosene" by Big Black.

Lilly Cahill and William Carlisle are alone in the library.

It's Monday, 6th October.

It's 8:31 A.M.

WILLIAM. When did you arrive?
LILLY. Last week.
WILLIAM. Whereabouts are you living?
LILLY. In Heaton Moor.
WILLIAM. Whereabouts in Heaton Moor?
LILLY. At the top of Broad Stone Road. By the nursery there.
WILLIAM. That's a nice street.
LILLY. I think so.
WILLIAM. Is it very different here?
LILLY. It is a bit.
WILLIAM. Have you settled in yet?
LILLY. I don't know.
WILLIAM. It must be slightly disorientating having to adjust to a new town in such a short space of time, is it?
LILLY. It's not too bad. I'm used to moving about.
WILLIAM. Why?

LILLY. My dad's worked in four different universities in the past twelve years. I've grown immune to it.

WILLIAM. Was Cambridge the best?

LILLY. Not really.

WILLIAM. Were the people there unthinkably intelligent?

LILLY. No. They were rude horrible pigs.

WILLIAM. Did they have enormous foreheads and big bulging brains.

LILLY. No. They were really rich and stupid.

WILLIAM. I want to go to Cambridge.

LILLY. Do you.

WILLIAM. That or Oxford. It's my life's ambition. How did you get here?

LILLY. What?

WILLIAM. What mode of transport did you use? To get to Stockport I mean. Not to school. Although you can tell me what mode of transport you used to get to school if you'd prefer.

LILLY. We drove.

WILLIAM. With everything packed in the car or did you hire a removal company?

LILLY. We hired a removal company. We had some things packed in the car.

WILLIAM. I like your haircut.

LILLY. Thanks.

WILLIAM. Is that coat real fur?

LILLY. No.

WILLIAM. It's faux?

LILLY. That's right.

WILLIAM. That's a relief.

LILLY. Yeah.

WILLIAM. It'd be terrible if you were some kind of animal killer. Imagine my embarrassment.

LILLY. I'm not.

WILLIAM. The fur trade's abominable. People who wear fur coats should be skinned alive in my opinion.

LILLY. Mine too.

WILLIAM. Good. I'm glad. I'm William.

LILLY. Hi William.

WILLIAM. I've been coming here for five years. I know the place completely inside-out. I know every nook and cranny and everything so if you want any help.

LILLY. Great.

WILLIAM. I know parts of this school that other people don't even know exist. There are secret corridors. Deserted book cupboards. Cellars. Attics. All kinds of things. You want to know about them? Just ask me. This is the Upper School library. Don't you love it?

LILLY. It's —

WILLIAM. It's completely hermetically sealed from the rest of the school. They tell us it's to keep the Lower School away. I think it's to keep us contained. Look outside.

LILLY. Where?

WILLIAM. That track leads up to Manchester in that direction and all the way down to London in that direction. The trains come past here all the time. They need to keep us locked in in case we escape.

Most of the Sixth Form can't be bothered to come up here anymore. They go to the common room. Or to the main library. They spend hour after hour after hour on the internet there. I prefer it here. It's intimate.

Do you know where to go to eat?

LILLY. I was going to go to the canteen.

WILLIAM. Don't. You mustn't. Nobody goes there. You'll die very quickly if you start eating your lunches there. *(She breaks into a smile.)* I'm being serious. *(Bennett Francis and Cissy Franks enter.)*

BENNETT. And this monkey is stood on the bus yelling at all the little Year Seven babies about how he'd stopped smoking and so anybody who smoked that day was getting glassed before they got off the bus. I looked at him. Pulled three cigarettes out. Lit them all at once. Smoked them.

CISSY. All in one go?

BENNETT. Oh yes.

CISSY. Didn't that hurt?

BENNETT. Viciously.

CISSY. It doesn't look as though he glassed you.

BENNETT. Of course he didn't glass me. He likes my arse too much. How was the rest of your evening?

CISSY. It passed.

BENNETT. How was your dad?

CISSY. You know. The same. I wish you'd stayed.

BENNET. Yes. *(Notices Lilly.)* Who the fuck are you?

WILLIAM. Bennett this is Lilly Cahill.

BENNETT. Is it?

WILLIAM. She's new.

BENNETT. Are you?

WILLIAM. This morning.

CISSY. Is she? *(Pause. They look at her. William awaits their verdict.)*

BENNETT. Did we hear about you?

LILLY. I've no idea.

WILLIAM. There was an email.

BENNETT. I bet there was. There's always an email. I'm Bennett.

LILLY. Hello Bennett.

BENNETT. Cahill's a very good name.

LILLY. Is it?

BENNETT. It's Irish. From County Galway. It's ancient.

LILLY. Right.

CISSY. I'm Cissy.

LILLY. Hello.

WILLIAM. Cissy's Bennett's girlfriend.

LILLY. Great.

CISSY. You're not from round here are you?

WILLIAM. She's from Cambridge.

CISSY. I can tell. From your accent.

BENNETT. She's shatteringly astute like that.

WILLIAM. Yeah. You have to get up really fucking early in the morning to catch her out. *(Beat.)*

BENNETT. How long are you here for?

LILLY. I don't know. Until the exams I think.

BENNETT. Brilliant.

CISSY. What are you taking?

LILLY. Geography, History, French, and English.

BENNETT. Four A-Levels?

WILLIAM. She's incredibly clever.

CISSY. Clearly.

LILLY. And General Studies.

BENNETT. Yes. Everybody takes General Studies. Nobody goes. Ever.

WILLIAM. I do.

BENNETT. What's Cambridge like?

WILLIAM. You should too. It's Mr. Lloyd. He's great.

LILLY. I hated it.

CISSY. That's good.

LILLY. Why?

CISSY. I only really trust people who hate their hometowns.

WILLIAM. Me too.

CISSY. How are you this morning William Carlisle?

WILLIAM. I'm fantastically fucking brilliant thank you very much for asking. How are you Cissy?

CISSY. Great. Happy to be here. Happy as a song lark.

WILLIAM. Good weekend?

CISSY. Thrilling. We had a dinner party on Saturday night. Bennett cooked a salmon. My mother swooned. How was yours?

WILLIAM. Terrible. Far, far better here. *(Nicholas Chatman enters. He is drinking a protein drink.)*

LILLY. Why was it terrible?

BENNETT. Shit. I've forgotten everything.

WILLIAM. What?

NICHOLAS. You'll never believe what I saw on Sunday.

LILLY. Why was your weekend terrible?

CISSY. What do you mean you've forgotten everything?

WILLIAM. You're better off not knowing. Seriously.

BENNETT. My English books, my French books, my History books. The works. What did you see?

NICHOLAS. *Deep Throat.*

BENNETT. Bless.

CISSY. What are you going to do without your books?

BENNETT. Lie. Busk it. Copy yours. Steal theirs. I've not seen that film in years and years and years.

CISSY. I've never seen it.

NICHOLAS. You should do. It's extraordinary.

LILLY. Why?

NICHOLAS. What?

LILLY. Why's it extraordinary?

WILLIAM. Lilly, this is Nicholas Chatman. He plays lacrosse. Nicholas this is Lilly. She's from Cambridge. She's new. *(Nicholas assesses her before he answers her question.)*

NICHOLAS. Right. *(Bennett interrupts him before he's able to.)*

BENNETT. I like your jacket, Mr Chatman.

NICHOLAS. Thank you very much Mr Francis.

CISSY. Can I try it on?

NICHOLAS. What?

CISSY. Your jacket. Can I? Please.

BENNETT. Is it Paul Smith?

NICHOLAS. Moschino.

CISSY. It's lovely.

BENNETT. It looks better on Nicholas.

WILLIAM. What's your first lesson?

LILLY. Geography. Period 2.

CISSY. Can I keep it?

NICHOLAS. No. Don't be ridiculous.

WILLIAM. Who with?

LILLY. Harrison.

WILLIAM. I've got him, then.

LILLY. What's he like?

CISSY. It smells lovely. It smells all manly. *(Tanya Gleason enters.)*

WILLIAM. He's a little unsettling. He's generally fine.

TANYA. *(Stops and looks at Lilly.)* Are you Lilly?

LILLY. That's right.

TANYA. I'm Tanya.

LILLY. Hello.

TANYA. Tanya Gleason? MacFarlane asked me to meet you. Did she not say?

LILLY. I'm not sure.

TANYA. I thought you were going to be in the common room. How did you get up here?

LILLY. I just walked.

TANYA. She wanted me to look after you today.

LILLY. To look after me?

TANYA. I've been looking for you for a while.

LILLY. I'm sorry.

TANYA. We had an email about you.

LILLY. Did you?

TANYA. Last Friday. It said you were starting today. That you were coming from Cambridge. That your father was working in the university. That we should be especially nice to you.

LILLY. Why did it say that?

TANYA. I have no idea. They send us these things. I think they're all a bit dysfunctional. I like your hair. *(She smiles. Comes properly into the room.)*

LILLY. My hair?

TANYA. It's quite Florence and the Machine. I noticed something about Year Seven kids.

CISSY. You noticed something about what?

TANYA. About the children in Year Seven.

CISSY. When?

TANYA. This morning.

CISSY. You're very random sometimes Tanya, sweetheart, I have to say.

TANYA. When they line up. If you push them. They all fall on top of one another. Like little toys.

CISSY. That's really mean. They could break their little bones.

TANYA. We were never as rude as they are. I was terrified of Sixth Formers. I was quite literally frozen with fear. I used to think they threw bricks at you. Flushed your head down the toilet. Set fire to your tie.

NICHOLAS. Can I ask you a question?

BENNETT. I've a feeling you're going to, aren't you?

NICHOLAS. Have you started revising yet?

BENNETT. Are you being serious?

NICHOLAS. I kind of am, actually.

BENNETT. Oh my Lord alive!

TANYA. They're only mocks. You don't need to revise for mocks.

CISSY. I never need to. I never need to revise for anything. I just do the exams.

BENNETT. And get As. You tart.

WILLIAM. It defeats the point of mocks if you revise for them. They're a dip-stick of what stage you're at, educationally, at this particular moment, intended to help you get a handle on how much revision you need to do from this point onwards as you move towards the final exams. *(They look at him for a beat.)*

NICHOLAS. 'Cause I've started.

BENNETT. You would have done. Swot.

NICHOLAS. It's not about being a swot.

BENNETT. Yeah it is.

NICHOLAS. It isn't. It's about wanting to do my best.

CISSY. My mum would kill me if I got less than an A in any subject.

WILLIAM. Would she literally kill you?

CISSY. Yes. Literally. She'd burn me alive.

BENNETT. When do they start, exactly? *(Beat.)*

CISSY. Are you serious?

BENNETT. Don't I look it?

CISSY. You don't know when the mocks start?

BENNETT. You never believe me about these kinds of things.

CISSY. November 3rd. 8:50 A.M. Main Hall. French. 11:55. Main Hall, Geography. 2:05 P.M. Back Pitch PE. Finishing Monday 10th, 2:05 P.M., Main Hall, History.

TANYA. You don't do PE.

BENNETT. Does anybody?

TANYA. How do you know when the PE exam is when you don't even do PE?

CISSY. I memorised it. I've got a photographic memory.

NICHOLAS. I like your badge. *(A pause.)*

LILLY. Thank you.

NICHOLAS. I like the White Stripes. They're fucking great.

LILLY. I think so too.

WILLIAM. He's only got two albums.

LILLY. What?

WILLIAM. Nicholas. He's only got two White Stripes albums. He only got *Elephant* last term. He doesn't even have *White Blood Cells*. Have you?

NICHOLAS. What?

WILLIAM. Have you ever even heard *White Blood Cells*?

NICHOLAS. What are you talking about?

WILLIAM. See. *(Chadwick Meade enters. He's wearing a new coat.)*

BENNETT. Holy fucking moly on a horse it's Kanye West!

CHADWICK. Who?

BENNETT. Have you ever set fire to a tie Chadwick?

CHADWICK. No.

BENNETT. I should think not. With a coat like that who fucking knows what might happen?

WILLIAM. Chadwick, this is Lilly.

CHADWICK. Lilly?

WILLIAM. Lilly Cahill. She's joining our school. She came from Cambridge. Lilly this is Chadwick Meade.

LILLY. Hello.

CHADWICK. Hello Lilly. I'm sorry. I wasn't expecting a new girl. It's terribly nice to meet you. Welcome to the school. I hope you are very happy here.

LILLY. Thank you Chadwick.

CHADWICK. Whereabouts in Cambridge are you from?

LILLY. Burwell.

CHADWICK. With the castle.

LILLY. That's right.

CHADWICK. Built under King Stephen. During the Anarchy. I like Cambridge.

LILLY. Do you?

CHADWICK. I prefer it to Oxford. Not only for its beauty but I think the university is better. Certainly in its Applied Mathematics department. Which is my specialism. My hero worked at St Johns in the twenties. Paul Dirac. Did you ever hear of him?

LILLY. I didn't I'm afraid.

BENNETT. Chadwick who the fuck ever heard of Paul Dirac?

CHADWICK. He predicted the existence of anti-matter. He developed the Dirac Equation which described the behaviour of electrons. He won the Nobel Prize in 1933. He said "the laws of nature should be expressed in beautiful equations." He's fundamental to the way we perceive the world. He was at Cambridge.

LILLY. I don't know him.

CHADWICK. He died in 1984.

WILLIAM. Nearly fifteen years before she was born, Chadwick you could hardly blame her, pal.

LILLY. Is that really your name, Chadwick?

CHADWICK. Yes it is, I'm afraid. It's American in origin.

TANYA. I didn't believe him either if that's any consolation. I thought he made it up.

BENNETT. I think he made his head up. Who christened you Chadwick, Chadwick? Which parent?

CHADWICK. I wasn't christened. My parents are atheists.

BENNETT. I *bet* they're atheists. You'd have to be with a son like that.

CISSY. With a face like that.

BENNETT. *(Turns to Chadwick.)* Stun me.

CHADWICK. What?

BENNETT. Stun me Chadwick. Tell me something stunning. Tell me something the like of which I've never even thought possible before. *(The others look at Chadwick.)*

CHADWICK. Do you know how many galaxies there are in the universe? About a hundred billion. And there are about a hundred billion stars in most given galaxies. That's ten thousand billion billion stars in the universe. Which works out as about ten million billion billion planets. *(The others look at Bennett.)*

BENNETT. It's like having an absurdly clever puppy.

NICHOLAS. Has anybody seen Copley, by the way?

CISSY. The new teacher?

NICHOLAS. She's not a teacher.

BENNETT. Course she's a fucking teacher. What is she if she's not a teacher? The traffic lady?

NICHOLAS. She's a student.

BENNETT. Yes.

NICHOLAS. Students don't count. I'm going to ask her out. *(Beat.)*

TANYA. Are you really going to ask a teacher out?

NICHOLAS. Why not? She's only about six months older than me I reckon. She came with us to *Macbeth*. She sat next to me. She's having a torturous time with Year Nine. She kept asking my advice.

BENNETT. Nicholas. You're gorgeous. Did you know that? Gorgeous!

WILLIAM. Are you incredibly nervous about coming to our school?

LILLY. No.

WILLIAM. You shouldn't be.

LILLY. I'm not.

CISSY. Unless you get frightened of being bored.

TANYA. Yeah.

CISSY. Because it is quite fucking stupefyingly boring.

WILLIAM. It's not that bad. Don't listen to her. Sometimes it is. *(The bell goes.)*

CISSY. That's my curtain call suckers.

BENNETT. What have you got?

CISSY. Double maths.

BENNETT. You've always got double maths. I'm not entirely sure it can be good for you. *(Cissy kisses him. He doesn't kiss her back. Tanya stands to leave.)*

CISSY. Where are you going?

TANYA. English.

CISSY. A bit early aren't you?

TANYA. I'm going to see Mr Anderson.

BENNETT. Are you going to ask him to impregnate you?

TANYA. What?

BENNETT. Cissy told me about your fantasy. Did you hear this Nicholas? Tanya's biggest dream is to live with Anderson. To be his secret lover. To have his baby. To waddle about his flat barefoot and pregnant. She's absolutely serious about it by the way.

TANYA. Fuck off.

BENNETT. Aren't you?

TANYA. Did you say that to him?

14

CISSY. I don't believe you Bennett.

BENNETT. It's true. Am I lying? Are you calling me a liar?

TANYA. Cissy. How could — ? *(Goes to say something. Nearly starts crying. Says nothing. Leaves.)*

CISSY. Tanya! Tanya wait! *(Follows after her. The rest listen to her calling down the corridor.)*

LILLY. I need to go and see Mr Eldridge.

WILLIAM. Do you know where he is?

LILLY. He's in his office. I was there earlier. It's just down the corridor isn't it?

WILLIAM. Second left after the common room.

LILLY. That's right.

WILLIAM. Right then.

LILLY. Good.

WILLIAM. I'll see you in Geography then probably.

LILLY. Yes. Probably. Where is that again?

WILLIAM. J-3. Do you know how to get there?

LILLY. I haven't got a clue. If I come back here can I go with you?

WILLIAM. Of course you can.

LILLY. Are you sure?

WILLIAM. It would be a pleasure. I don't mind at all.

LILLY. Thanks. Thank you William. I'll be here at about half past.

WILLIAM. Perfect. I'll take you the scenic route.

LILLY. Is it always this cold in here?

WILLIAM. Always. Until they put the heating on. Then it's insufferably hot.

LILLY. I look forward to that.

WILLIAM. Have fun with Eldridge.

LILLY. I will do. I'll see you in a bit.

WILLIAM. Yeah. See you in a bit.

LILLY. See you in a bit Bennett. Nicholas.

BENNETT. See you Florence.

WILLIAM. Fuck off Bennett. Leave her alone. *(Lilly smiles at William, then turns to Nicholas.)*

LILLY. See you.

NICHOLAS. Bye. *(She leaves. Some time.)*

BENNETT. "I'll take you the scenic route." *(Bennett and Nicholas giggle at William.)* Can I ask you something Mr William Carlisle?

WILLIAM. Go on.

BENNETT. Have you ever actually had a girlfriend before?

WILLIAM. What are you talking about?
BENNETT. Have you?
WILLIAM. What do you want to know that for?
BENNETT. You haven't have you? I find that quite touching.
WILLIAM. Piss off Bennett.
BENNETT. You're a bit besotted mate aren't you? She'll break your heart William.
WILLIAM. I don't know what you're wittering on about.
BENNETT. *(Looks at him. Smiles.)* No.

Scene 2

"Eric's Trip" by Sonic Youth.

It's 3:30 P.M. Tuesday, October 14th.

Lilly and William are in the library.

LILLY. Do you know what I've noticed about you? You're very still. You stand very still most of the time. You move your head quite slowly. I really like it. I like your hair too.
WILLIAM. Thanks.
LILLY. It looks shy. You've got shy hair. *(William smiles. Looks away slightly.)* How was History?
WILLIAM. It was unusually dramatic. We had Lloyd. He was in a peculiar mood. He came in. We were sitting down. He looked at us for about three seconds. He sat down. We were all chatting. He looked at us. We kept chatting. He looked some more. We chatted some more. He sat still. We chatted. He waited until we stopped. And then he waited until we were silent. This took about a minute. And then he just waited. He waited five more minutes. Said he had decided not to teach us today. He didn't think we deserved it. Until we said sorry to him. And we did. One by one. Went round the class. "Sorry sir. Sorry sir."
LILLY. Is he your favourite?
WILLIAM. I think so. I find his classroom management skills rather bracing.

LILLY. Have you finished your UCAS form? *(William nods.)* Have you sent it off?

WILLIAM. This morning. Have you?

LILLY. I'm doing it tonight.

WILLIAM. You better had.

LILLY. Are you applying for a year off?

WILLIAM. Christ no.

LILLY. Every other fucker is.

WILLIAM. I can't wait. Just to get out.

LILLY. No. Me neither. *(Looks at him. Her gaze unnerves him a little.)*

WILLIAM. How was French?

LILLY. *Un cauchemar sociologique.*

WILLIAM. *Un* whatty what what?

LILLY. Do you ever worry about Chadwick Meade?

WILLIAM. You're losing me.

LILLY. He's in our French lesson. He's a brilliant linguist. He never says a word. He was rocking for most of the lesson. Ever so slightly. I was sitting next to him. It really unsettled me.

WILLIAM. Rocking?

LILLY. To and fro.

WILLIAM. That sounds rather comforting.

LILLY. It was weird. I'm not entirely sure I trust him. I'm not sure I like him.

WILLIAM. What's not to like? He's the cleverest man in the universe.

LILLY. He's not normal.

WILLIAM. I hate normal people. Normal people should be eviscerated. He has a monster of a time. He's on a rather considerable scholarship. You should be nice to him.

LILLY. I hate the word "should."

WILLIAM. The pressure he gets. The thoughts he has. People should be careful around him.

LILLY. That was kind of my point.

WILLIAM. One day he's going to snap, I think.

LILLY. What do you mean?

WILLIAM. He's too timid half the time. He should stand up to it. Stick his chin out. I wish he would. I've seen it happen.

LILLY. Seen what happen?

WILLIAM. People like him who get so much abuse and then one day. Pop.

LILLY. Pop?

WILLIAM. I like him.

LILLY. I'm glad somebody does.

WILLIAM. We went to Cambridge University together in the summer holidays. On a visit. He's a lot funnier when you get him on his own. I think he gets nervous of speaking too much in front of people like Bennett. People notice him because of his scholarship tie. He said that it's a constant reminder. He took me to where Isaac Newton studied. He took me to the Botanic Gardens there. Showed me a tree which is apparently a descendent of the apple tree that Newton sat under.

It was unlike anything I've ever seen.

We went to King's. Which is the college I've applied for. Asked somebody where we should go and look. There was a doctor in there. A scientist. Somebody with, he had a white coat on. He told me we should go and look at the chapel there. He said it was rather beautiful. I'd never heard a man use the word beautiful like that before.

It was beautiful, by the way. Parts of it date from the middle of the fifteenth century. The ceiling is spectacular. It has rather breathtaking fan vaulting. It was designed by Wastell. And built by him, actually.

If my application's accepted I'll have my interview next month. I hope I get one, an interview. They do the mock interviews in here. Lloyd does them. It'd be great. Just me and Lloyd. In here. Having an interview!

It's half three. We should be going home.

LILLY. Yeah.

WILLIAM. It's amazing how quickly this whole place empties. I love it. I love being here when it does. You walk down the whole corridor and you're the only one there.

This room becomes like a kind of cocoon.

It's cold today. It feels like it's turning into autumn. I always think you can feel the exact day when that happens in this country.

Can I ask you: How are you getting on?

LILLY. What do you mean?

WILLIAM. Here. How was your first week?

LILLY. It was all right. It was a bit odd. Some of the teachers are a bit strange. It's strange that there are so few of us. It can feel a bit claustrophobic. Bennett does my head in occasionally.

WILLIAM. What I meant was: What do you think of Stockport?

LILLY. *(Thinks.)* Honestly?

WILLIAM. Honestly.

LILLY. I've been to worse places. I've lived in worse places. Heaton Moor's nice. We went to Lyme Park at the weekend. It was gorgeous.

WILLIAM. The deer park there's medieval. If you move slowly enough there are fallow deer there that let you stroke them.

LILLY. The shopping centre in town makes me want to gouge my eyes out, though.

WILLIAM. Ha!

LILLY. And I hate all the people. *(Pause.)*

WILLIAM. All of them?

LILLY. Apart from you lot, here.

WILLIAM. You hate all of the people you've met in Stockport?

LILLY. Yeah. *(He looks at her.)*

WILLIAM. With their tied-back hair. And their stupid ugly makeup and their burgers?

LILLY. And their faces. *(They smile at each other.)*

WILLIAM. "What the fuck are you looking at?"

LILLY. "I'm looking at you, you Chav shit."

WILLIAM. I know what you mean.

LILLY. Pound-stretcher store-card holders the lot of them.

WILLIAM. And all the boys are fathers at seventeen and banned from being within a square mile of their children at nineteen and jailed at twenty-one.

LILLY. They deserve it.

WILLIAM. Because they're thick and they're vicious.

LILLY. And they're fat and they're ugly.

WILLIAM. And frightened of anything that's different from what they're like.

LILLY. And terrified of intelligence or thought.

WILLIAM. They're nervous about thinking because if they think too much they might just realise that the way they live their lives with their shell suits and their vicious little ugly little dogs is not necessarily the only way to lead a life.

LILLY. And they can't fucking wait till Christmas. And the furthest they've ever been to is Spain.

WILLIAM. And even then they hated it.

LILLY. And wanted to eat more egg and chips.

WILLIAM. Do you know something?

LILLY. What?

WILLIAM. I always thought I was the only person who thought those kind of thoughts.

Can I tell you: I sometimes think I'm the best person in this town. Is that terrible?

LILLY. No.

WILLIAM. I'm definitely the cleverest. And the funniest. Don't you think?

LILLY. *(Thinks.)* Yeah.

WILLIAM. Do you?

LILLY. Yeah.

WILLIAM. I do too. I think I'm hilarious. Do you ever think about the person you wished you were?

LILLY. Sometimes.

WILLIAM. When I think of that person, do you know what I realise?

LILLY. What?

WILLIAM. I realise I *am* him.

Can I ask you? Do Bennett and Nicholas and Cissy ever say anything about me?

LILLY. No.

WILLIAM. Never?

LILLY. No.

WILLIAM. Do they never talk about my family?

LILLY. No.

WILLIAM. Or my job?

Have they told you about my job?

LILLY. What job's that? *(Pause. He has to stop himself from chuckling a little, which makes her chuckle a little too.)*

WILLIAM. If I told you, you wouldn't believe me.

LILLY. Go on.

WILLIAM. Nobody believes me.

LILLY. I would.

WILLIAM. Why?

LILLY. What do you mean?

WILLIAM. Why would you believe me when nobody else in their right mind would?

LILLY. I'm very trusting.

WILLIAM. I bet you are.

LILLY. What?

WILLIAM. I said I bet you are. *(Stops chuckling and becomes suddenly serious. She can't stop so quickly.)* I work for the government.

LILLY. Do you?

WILLIAM. See?

LILLY. What?

WILLIAM. You don't believe me.

LILLY. I never said that. Of course I believe you.

WILLIAM. Then you're mad.

LILLY. Why?

WILLIAM. As if a seventeen-year-old would work for the government!

LILLY. You told me you did. I believe you. Even if you try and deny it now I'll still believe you. *(Pause.)*

WILLIAM. It's covert.

LILLY. I'm sure.

WILLIAM. They don't tell anybody about it. People would get freaked out. They'd think I was a bit young.

LILLY. I can imagine. What do you do for them?

WILLIAM. I observe Muslim teenagers for them. They want to target Muslim teenagers. So obviously they employ a teenager to do it. It would be stupid to employ an adult. So actually they employed me.

LILLY. That sounds exciting.

WILLIAM. It isn't. Mostly Muslim teenagers are very boring. I have to fill in a brief form every fortnight.

LILLY. Have you cracked any terrorist rings?

WILLIAM. No. Mainly they play football and snog each other behind their parents' backs. *(The two giggle together.)* Can I ask you something?

LILLY. Anything.

WILLIAM. How many hours do you normally sleep?

LILLY. Sorry?

WILLIAM. On average? Every night?

LILLY. Nine.

WILLIAM. Nine?

LILLY. Ten sometimes. Eleven if I get an early night.

WILLIAM. Right.

LILLY. Twelve on a weekend.

WILLIAM. I sleep four. Can I ask you something else?

LILLY. Of course you can?

WILLIAM. Don't you ever get frightened? *(She looks at him, thinks before she answers.)*

LILLY. Yes I do. *(He thinks before he presses her.)*

WILLIAM. Tell me what kind of things you get frightened of?

LILLY. *(Thinks.)* Nuclear war.

Black people.

Dogs. Most dogs. Some birds. Farm animals.

Sexual assault.

I get frightened of waking up in my house and there's somebody there in my room.

Sometimes in the middle of the night when my parents go out my mum storms off. She walks home, comes home early. Really drunk. My bedroom's downstairs. It always is. For the last three houses. I prefer it … She normally forgets her keys so she normally taps on my window to get me to let her in. I sometimes think it's dead people outside. That terrifies me.

WILLIAM. What does she storm off for?

LILLY. She gets pissed off at my dad. She drinks two bottles of wine.

WILLIAM. My mum died when I was about four.

I don't really remember her. I never knew my dad. My dad died before I was born.

I don't tell anybody that. That's a secret. Can I trust you to keep that to yourself?

LILLY. Of course you can.

WILLIAM. Thanks.

LILLY. Do you remember her dying?

WILLIAM. A little bit.

LILLY. What do you remember about it?

WILLIAM. I remember the police in our living room drinking tea. The police came round for some reason. I remember one of them had four sugars. I remember her funeral. Everybody patted me a lot.

LILLY. So you're a little orphan boy.

WILLIAM. That's right.

LILLY. I wouldn't feel too sorry for yourself by the way.

WILLIAM. I don't.

LILLY. Parents can be complete shits.

WILLIAM. I'm sure. What are those scars? On your arm? *(She looks at him before she answers.)*

LILLY. What do you think they are?

WILLIAM. Do you cut yourself?

LILLY. You're cute.

WILLIAM. Do you Lilly?

LILLY. Watch this. *(She pulls out a Bic lighter. She lights it. She keeps it lit for ages until the metal on it is roasting hot. She turns it off. She burns a smiley into her arm with the metal on the top of the lighter.)*

WILLIAM. Does that hurt?

LILLY. No. It feels really nice. *(He watches her finish it off. She shows it to him.)*

WILLIAM. Can I touch it? *(She looks at him for a beat. Then she nods. He does. She winces a bit.)* Have you felt how hot I am? Feel my forehead. *(She does.)* Do you know what I think?

LILLY. What do you think William Carlisle?

WILLIAM. I think our bodies are machines. *(He moves away from her. Breaking her touch.)*

You know where the heat from our body comes from. It comes from the energy it burns up carrying out all of its different activities. That's why corpses are so cold. Because the machine has stopped.

LILLY. I'm not a machine. I'm an animal.

WILLIAM. What kind of animal are you?

LILLY. A wolf. A leopard. A rhinoceros. A gazelle. A cheetah. An eagle. A snake.

WILLIAM. I feel like I've known you for years.

LILLY. You haven't.

WILLIAM. When we were little did we go on holiday together or something like that?

LILLY. I don't think so William.

WILLIAM. I think we did. Did we go camping together?

LILLY. No.

WILLIAM. What school did you go to when you were little?

LILLY. St Michael's in Tunbridge Wells.

WILLIAM. It can't have been that then.

Would you like to go out with me?

LILLY. Go out with you?

WILLIAM. On a date. We could go to the theatre. Or I could take you out for a meal.

LILLY. A meal?

WILLIAM. Even though I hate restaurants.

LILLY. You hate them?

WILLIAM. They scare the life out of me.

LILLY. Why?

WILLIAM. All those people watching you eat.

LILLY. Why would you take me there then?

WILLIAM. We could go to the cinema then. Or bowling. Swimming.

LILLY. Swimming?

WILLIAM. Have you ever been to Chapel?

LILLY. To where?

WILLIAM. Chapel-en-le-Frith? It's a village. In Derbyshire. It's somewhere else that's beautiful. We could go next week. In the half term, if you'd like to. We can get a train.

Would you like to?

Would you like to go out with me at all?

LILLY. I don't think so. *(A beat.)*

WILLIAM. Right.

LILLY. I don't really want to go out with anybody at the moment.

WILLIAM. Right.

LILLY. It's absolutely not you so don't think that. I just can't be doing with a fucking boyfriend.

WILLIAM. No.

LILLY. I'm sorry. *(Pause.)*

WILLIAM. I've never done that before.

LILLY. What?

WILLIAM. Asked anybody out.

It didn't really go very well did it?

LILLY. It wasn't —

WILLIAM. I really fucked it up.

LILLY. No. You did all right.

WILLIAM. Disappointing outcome though I have to say. A complete embarrassment if the truth be told.

LILLY. I don't think it was. I think it was romantic.

Scene 3

"Loose" by the Stooges.

12:46 P.M. Thursday, 30th October.

Lilly and Nicholas are in the common room.

LILLY. Hi.

NICHOLAS. Hi.

LILLY. How's it going in there?

NICHOLAS. It's going OK. How are you getting on? *(Lilly nods her head at him for a while. Smiles. Says nothing.)*

LILLY. How's the revision?

NICHOLAS. You know.

LILLY. You ready yet?

NICHOLAS. Oh. I think so.

LILLY. Have you seen William?

NICHOLAS. Not this morning. Not all day.

LILLY. He's not been in since the break.

NICHOLAS. I didn't notice.

LILLY. Are you coming out for lunch?

NICHOLAS. I'm going to the gym. *(She looks at him.)*

LILLY. Come here. *(He does.)* Take your blazer off. *(He does.)* Flex your muscles. *(He does. She strokes them.)* Thank you. *(She takes an apple out of her bag. Eats it.)* Do you want an apple? I've got a spare one.

NICHOLAS. I'm all right.

LILLY. He asked me out. William.

NICHOLAS. When?

LILLY. Before half term.

NICHOLAS. What did you say?

LILLY. What do you think?

NICHOLAS. I don't know. Hence me asking.

LILLY. He was really funny. His face went all stupid. I did feel a bit sorry for him.

NICHOLAS. Why?

LILLY. Have you ever noticed that?

NICHOLAS. Noticed what?

LILLY. When you think somebody's a complete dick you find out something about them and you can't help feeling sorry for them even if you really don't want to.

NICHOLAS. What did you find out about William?

LILLY. He told me about his mum.

 Has he ever talked to you about her?

NICHOLAS. Not really. Not much. We're not that close. What did he say about her?

LILLY. She's dead. Did you know that?

 His dad died before he was born.

 She died when he was little.

 He was four. Imagine that.

NICHOLAS. Did he tell you that, did he?

LILLY. Imagine being four years old and watching your mum die. You have to admit it's a bit heartbreaking.

NICHOLAS. Is that what he said to you? That his parents were dead? *(Pause.)*

LILLY. Aren't they?

NICHOLAS. When did he say that?

LILLY. Two weeks ago. When he asked me —

 They're not are they?

NICHOLAS. His dad's an accountant. His mum's a nursery school teacher in Cheadle. She's lovely. She looks really young for a mum. She's quite attractive as it goes.

LILLY. Fuck.

NICHOLAS. Yeah.

LILLY. That's quite unsettling.

NICHOLAS. I know.

LILLY. I'm quite unsettled now.

 You've unsettled me.

NICHOLAS. I didn't intend to.

LILLY. Why would he lie about something like that?

NICHOLAS. I've no idea.

 He had a brother. I think this is true. I think he had a brother who died. When he was just a little kid.

 Maybe he was —

LILLY. What?

NICHOLAS. I don't know.

LILLY. Confused? You can't get confused about something like that. You can't mistake one for the other.

He was doing it for attention.

How selfish can you get? I'm tempted to find where he lives and go round and tell them.

NICHOLAS. Don't.

LILLY. No.

NICHOLAS. Hey.

LILLY. Hey.

I've been thinking about you all morning. Did you know that?

NICHOLAS. No.

LILLY. Well it's true. And I have to say that some of the things I've been thinking are a bit filthy. *(He goes to her. Kisses her on the lips.)*

NICHOLAS. I've been thinking about you, too.

LILLY. Liar.

NICHOLAS. Last night.

LILLY. Yeah? What about it? *(Some time.)*

NICHOLAS. Can I confess something?

LILLY. Go on.

NICHOLAS. I'd never had sex before.

LILLY. Right.

NICHOLAS. Could you tell?

What?

What are you laughing at?

LILLY. Men. Boys. They're so …

NICHOLAS. What?

LILLY. Nothing. No. I couldn't tell. I didn't care.

NICHOLAS. It was fucking amazing.

LILLY. It was a bit, wasn't it?

NICHOLAS. You were fucking amazing.

LILLY. Chump.

NICHOLAS. Well. It's true.

Lilly.

LILLY. Nicholas.

NICHOLAS. I don't think we should tell anybody.

LILLY. What?

NICHOLAS. I think we should keep it to ourselves. That we're going out with one another. I think it'd probably be best if people didn't know.

LILLY. Why?

NICHOLAS. Don't you think?

LILLY. I don't know.

NICHOLAS. People here are so —

LILLY. What?

NICHOLAS. They just go on and on.

LILLY. Are you ashamed of me?

NICHOLAS. No. Don't be stupid.

LILLY. I'm not being stupid in the least.

NICHOLAS. I'm not saying that.

LILLY. You just want to keep me as your little secret?

NICHOLAS. Kind of.

LILLY. Prick.

NICHOLAS. What?

LILLY. You. You're a prick.

How are things going with Miss Copley?

NICHOLAS. Are you cross with me?

LILLY. Has she fallen for your overwhelming sexual aura yet Nicholas?

NICHOLAS. Have you got the slightest idea what people would say about you?

LILLY. Nicholas Chatman the Casanova of Nourishment. A million pheromones in every muscle.

NICHOLAS. Shut up.

LILLY. Honestly one fuck and he wishes he'd never met me.

Your face!

NICHOLAS. I'm going.

LILLY. Go and do your workout. Press those benches baby. Give them a squeeze from me.

NICHOLAS. Are you around later?

LILLY. Might be.

NICHOLAS. Lilly.

LILLY. I'm teasing. I'm sorry. Yes. I'm here later. I'll wait for you. And OK.

I won't tell anybody.

NICHOLAS. Thanks. I'm really sorry. I just think. Here. *(Kisses her.)* I'll see you later.

LILLY. See you later. *(He leaves. She sits. She looks at her apple. She picks a chunk out of it with her fingers. She eats it. She spits it out after a while. A train passes outside the window. She looks up to watch it. Cissy and Tanya enter. Cissy is eating a large chip sandwich.)*

CISSY. The amount of flour in this bread is fucking ridiculous.
Hi.
LILLY. Hi.
TANYA. Hi.
LILLY. Hi.
CISSY. What do you think these chips are made of?
TANYA. Dough, mainly.
CISSY. I shouldn't be having these. I don't even normally have lunch anymore. I just have Skittles. Have you ever had four packets of Skittles in one go. Your brain feels amazing. *(The girls smile at this idea. Some time.)*
TANYA. I think that's really dangerous. Human beings have to eat. It's one of the things that we do. Five pieces of fruit and veg a day. Regulated food groups. Thirty minutes exercise three times a week.
I blame the parents.
(The three girls burst out laughing. It takes them a while to recover.)
LILLY. Do you ever think about that?
TANYA. Think about what?
LILLY. Being a parent.
TANYA. All the time.
CISSY. She doesn't just mean about having Anderson's children. She means about actually properly being a parent.
TANYA. Yeah.
LILLY. Seriously?
TANYA. Seriously. *(A beat.)*
LILLY. Me too.
CISSY. God.
LILLY. I think I'd be a terrible mother.
TANYA. Don't be silly.
LILLY. My babies would probably all die. Really quickly. I wouldn't know how to feed them. I wouldn't know what to do with them. I'd end up putting them in a cupboard.
TANYA. You wouldn't.
LILLY. I would though.
CISSY. They can't remember anything until they're about five, anyway. You may as well put them in a cupboard. They wouldn't remember you doing it.
TANYA. I'm going to have four.
CISSY. Four?

TANYA. Yep. I'm going to be brilliant. Home-educate them. Take them to lots of sports meetings. In my big car.

CISSY. In Anderson's big car.

TANYA. In Anderson's big car.

LILLY. He hasn't got a big car. He comes to school on a bike.

TANYA. Tennis lessons. Football lessons. Ballet lessons. Anything they want. Teach them languages.

CISSY. You don't know any languages.

TANYA. I'd learn. Loads of languages and teach them all to our children.

You've got to admit he's fucking lovely.

Of course he's got a car. He just uses his bike to keep fit. And save the world.

(Pause. Cissy eats. Lilly takes a carrot from her bag and eats that.)

LILLY. Would you have Bennett's children?

CISSY. Fuck. Off.

LILLY. Why not?

CISSY. Can you imagine? They'd be impossible. *(They eat for a while. Lilly looks at her.)*

LILLY. What's he like?

CISSY. What do you mean?

LILLY. Bennett.

CISSY. What do you mean what's he like?

LILLY. You know.

CISSY. No.

LILLY. In bed.

CISSY. Oh Christ.

LILLY. What?

CISSY. I'd rather not go into that while I'm having my lunch. *(The girls chuckle together. Lilly watches Cissy.)* I'm not going to have children until I'm about forty-two. I'm going to wait until I can afford to pay for somebody else to look after them. I've got too many things I want to do. Too many places I want to go. I can't wait to leave England is one thing. Go and live abroad.

I'm going to. As soon as I finish here.

LILLY. Where are you going to go?

CISSY. Edinburgh. Glasgow. Dublin. Paris. Anywhere apart from here. *(Pause. Cissy wraps up her sandwich and puts it away. The other girls watch her.)* I'm so fat.

LILLY. You're not fat.

CISSY. Look at me.

LILLY. You're not fat. Don't say it because it's not true and it makes it look as if you're really showing off. *(Cissy looks at her. A beat.)*

CISSY. Yeah. *(Another beat. Cissy grins.)* What are you girls getting for Christmas? *(Bennett enters.)*

BENNETT. I'm getting really bored of Mahon telling me about gay heroes of literary history. She finds me every day. It's like she waits around corners for me and leaps out.

She makes me summarise articles from *The Guardian* for her.

CISSY. It's only because she's too thick to read them herself.

BENNETT. She keeps telling me that I could be a lawyer if I wanted to. I don't want to be a lawyer. Who wants to be a fucking lawyer for fucksake?

TANYA. Have you ever thought that there might be a reason?

BENNETT. What?

TANYA. That she singles you out for those kinds of suggestions?

BENNETT. What the fuck are you implying Miss Gleason?

TANYA. I'm not implying anything Mr Francis. I'm just asking a question.

BENNETT. Have they put the heating on?

This fucking room.

I need to get outside. I need to go and run around a bit. I need to do PE. I really miss PE. I never thought I'd say that, ever.

TANYA. I don't miss PE teachers.

BENNETT. That's because they're fucking retards.

CISSY. Apart from Cheetham.

BENNETT. He's a retard. He's a retardus primus.

CISSY. He was very sweet to me.

BENNETT. That's because he wanted to finger you.

CISSY. He told me he was really impressed with my GCSE results.

BENNETT. Yes, because he wanted to fucking finger you. I told you.

CISSY. Bennett.

BENNETT. Would you have let him?

CISSY. Don't.

BENNETT. I bet you would. Mind you I can't say I blame him. People get so het up about inter-generational sexual activity nowa-days. It's ridiculous. We should just all jolly well calm down I think. What's the youngest person you'd fuck Tanya? *(She looks at him. Glances at Cissy. Looks back at him.)* Sorry, you go in for the older man, do you not?

TANYA. Are you asking me about *my* sexual experiences Bennett? That's quite bold coming from you.

BENNETT. What does that mean? *(She smiles. Says nothing.)* I'd finger a Year Eight girl. If she was up for it. And if she wasn't I'd definitely have a bit of a posh wank thinking about her.

CISSY. Teachers shouldn't have sex. They're too old. I find it really unnerving. The idea of it. All that old skin. Wobbling about. *(Chadwick enters.)*

BENNETT. You always used to look forward to PE lessons didn't you Chadwick?

CHADWICK. What?

CISSY. Do you remember in swimming when he went diving for the brick? You nearly drowned didn't you sweetheart?

BENNETT. I remember him in the changing rooms. I remember his little tiny needle dick.

Chadwick.

TANYA. Here we go.

BENNETT. Is it true you squeeze lemon juice onto your hair? To make it go blonder?

CHADWICK. Sometimes.

BENNETT. Does it work?

CHADWICK. Yes.

TANYA. Does it?

CHADWICK. Yes.

BENNETT. You're a genius Chadwick I think aren't you. But you've got to admit.

CHADWICK. What?

BENNETT. You look pretty fucking stupid in that coat.

CHADWICK. Yeah.

BENNETT. Did you just actually agree with me?

TANYA. Shut up Bennett.

CISSY. Some people can wear a coat like that. Some people look like retards. *(William enters. He is frantic. He is drinking a red drink out of a mineral water bottle.)*

WILLIAM. Somebody's stolen my money. *(They look at him for a beat. He swigs.)*

TANYA. What money?

WILLIAM. I had about a hundred pounds.

TANYA. What did you have a hundred pounds for?

WILLIAM. It's not that much.

LILLY. Where have you been?

WILLIAM. What?

LILLY. You've not been in for days.

WILLIAM. What are you talking about?

TANYA. What did you bring a hundred pounds to school for?

WILLIAM. It was in my bag.

LILLY. When did you last see it?

WILLIAM. What do you mean when did I last see it? What kind of a fucking cunt of a question is that? "When did you last see it?" This morning. This morning is when I last saw it. I saw it this morning when I put it in there. Somebody's stolen it. People are always doing that to me.

TANYA. Are you sure?

WILLIAM. Don't I look like I'm sure?

TANYA. I make that kind of mistake all the time.

WILLIAM. Do I look like a liar?

TANYA. No. *(Moves towards him. He backs away from her suddenly.)*

WILLIAM. Were you trying to kiss me?

TANYA. What?

WILLIAM. Just then?

TANYA. No.

WILLIAM. Were you?

TANYA. No, I wasn't.

WILLIAM. "No, I wasn't." Is that why you moved closer to me.

TANYA. I didn't realise I did.

WILLIAM. People do that kind of thing though, don't they?

BENNETT. William. What are you drinking?

WILLIAM. *(Looks down at his drink.)* Campari and grapefruit juice. Do you want to try some?

BENNETT. Are you really?

WILLIAM. Why would I lie about something like that? It's my favourite drink for goodness sake. Here.

BENNETT. *(Takes it.)* Ta. *(Drinks.)* Wow. *(Drinks some more.)* Chadwick have you got any money on you?

CHADWICK. I'm sorry?

BENNETT. Have you Chadwick?

CHADWICK. What do you mean?

BENNETT. I mean have you got any money in your wallet or in your pocket or in your bag or up your arse that you could spare for

William. William's lost a hundred pounds and I think you should try and get it back to him, don't you?

CHADWICK. It's nothing to do with me.

BENNETT. I'm sorry?

CHADWICK. I said it's nothing to do with me.

BENNETT. Ha!

CHADWICK. William, I'm terribly sorry that you've lost some money but I don't really think it was my fault.

BENNETT. Chadwick. Get your wallet out.

TANYA. Bennett. Stop it. Now.

BENNETT. What? What Tanya? Are you actually trying to stop me here?

Chadwick get your wallet out fucking now you fucking cunt-faced twat or I will beat the fucking bricks out of your arse with my bare fists while everybody else watches and sings little fucking songs so help me God I will.

CHADWICK. Here.

BENNETT. How much is in there?

CHADWICK. Nothing.

BENNETT. How much you lying fuck.

CHADWICK. Twenty pounds.

BENNETT. Take it out.

CHADWICK. What?

BENNETT. Take it out of the wallet.

CHADWICK. No.

BENNETT. Now. Cunthead.

Thank you.

And give it to William. He's a bit short. *(Chadwick gives the money to William. Bennett watches. Has another drink. Silence. Some time. They all try not to move, apart from Bennett who moves with some comfort.)*

It's warmer today. I think. Don't you Chadwick? Haven't you noticed it's warmer today? They would put the heating on just as the sun comes out. How typical is that?

An Indian summer.

We're going to the dentist this afternoon. I've got the afternoon off. I'm looking forward to that. Hang out in the sunshine.

My mum's already here to collect me. I saw her. She's waiting in the reception. I decided to just walk straight past her.

Everybody's being very quiet.

How's the revision going Lilly? Have you started yet?

LILLY. Yes.

BENNETT. Sorry? You're muttering. I didn't hear you.

LILLY. I said yes. Of course I've started. The exams are next week.

BENNETT. *(Nods his head.)* Lovely. *(He goes to Chadwick. He stares at him. He touches his cheek.)*

What did you have this morning Chadders?

What subject did you have?

CHADWICK. Maths.

BENNETT. Maths. Very good. Very good. I had Politics. *(He burps in Chadwick's face. Lucy Francis enters. She's eleven. She is nervous in the room. The others notice her.)*

LUCY. Mum says you've got to hurry up.

BENNETT. *(Turns to Lucy.)* Right. Thank you Lucy. *(He collects his bag and jacket. He gives William his drink back. He stops right in front of Tanya.)* What's the matter with you?

TANYA. Nothing.

BENNETT. You look all sad. Are you really sad?

TANYA. No.

BENNETT. You are though, aren't you? Do you know why? Do you want to know why you're so sad? Should I tell you?

You're sad because you're fat.

You're fat because you eat too much.

You eat too much because you're depressed. You're depressed because of the fucking world.

Right. My dentist awaits these elegant gnashers. *(He gnashes his teeth at Chadwick. Leaves. The bell goes. They all wait for a beat. Lilly's looking at Cissy.)*

CISSY. What?

He was messing about.

Fucking hell. It was a joke.

He's just nervous. He's terrified of the dentist. Are you coming to English? *(Tanya looks at her. Says nothing.)* I'll walk with you. *(Tanya doesn't respond. Cissy exits.)*

TANYA. Are you OK?

CHADWICK. What?

TANYA. Are you OK, I asked.

CHADWICK. Of course. Yes. I'm fine. Of course I'm OK.

TANYA. I'm really sorry. I tried to stop him.

CHADWICK. Yes. I know. You don't need to tell me. *(Tanya looks at him for a second, then turns and leaves.)*

LILLY. What are you going to do?

About your money?

WILLIAM. Did you take it?

LILLY. What?

WILLIAM. I just wondered if you'd taken it. You might have done. You never know. You might have gone into my bag and found it.

LILLY. What are you talking about?

WILLIAM. Ha!

LILLY. What?

WILLIAM. Tricked you!

LILLY. You what?

WILLIAM. I'm just winding you up, Lilly. Just having a little joke. Do you want some of this? *(He drinks some more Campari and offers her the bottle.)*

LILLY. No thank you. I'll see you later.

WILLIAM. Yeah. I look forward to that. *(She leaves. Some time.)*

CHADWICK. How was your mock?

WILLIAM. It was good. It was Lloyd. He was very sharp. He's by some distance my favourite teacher. He gave me a cigarette at the end which was probably a bit unprofessional of him. But quite sweet as well.

When's yours?

CHADWICK. I'm not doing a mock. I'm just going to go down and do the interview.

WILLIAM. Right. *(Reaches into his own wallet and gives Chadwick the twenty pounds.)*

CHADWICK. Thank you.

WILLIAM. That's all right.

CHADWICK. He's —

WILLIAM. Yeah.

CHADWICK. I don't think I deserve some of the things that happen to me, you know?

Do you?

I don't think I'm so bad. I'm not as bad they make out. I'm not as stupid as people think.

WILLIAM. I don't think anybody thinks for a second that you're stupid in any way. *(Chadwick gets his phone out. He opens it. He finds a text. He reads it and shows it to William.)* When did you get this?

CHADWICK. This one came this morning.

WILLIAM. This isn't from Bennett is it?

CHADWICK. No. It's probably from somebody downstairs. That's why I come up here all the time.

WILLIAM. Have you had this kind of thing before?

You should tell somebody about it. This is serious Chadwick.

CHADWICK. Yeah.

Sometimes …

WILLIAM. What?

CHADWICK. Nothing.

WILLIAM. Go on. Chadwick, what were you going to say?

CHADWICK. There's far, far less anti-matter in the universe than there is matter. Did you know that?

WILLIAM. I'm not entirely sure that I did Chadwick, no. Was that really what you were going to say?

CHADWICK. Yes. That's one of the things that the experiments at CERN are investigating.

WILLIAM. CERN?

CHADWICK. The LHC?

The Large Hadron Collider?

(Chadwick's conviction stops William for a beat.)

One of the things that the experiments this Collider may be able to test is where all the anti-matter has gone to. Some people think that it must be somewhere. That it can't just disappear. Given its absence from the known universe they speculate that this proves that there are alternative universes. And that the anti-matter resides in these alternative universes.

I think the experiments there will prove them right.

If it was possible to harness anti-matter and to bring a single anti-matter positron into contact with a single electron of matter, it would create an explosion of untold force and energy. They could build an anti-matter bomb. It would be forty thousand times bigger than a nuclear bomb.

I think that'd be better.

Don't you think it'd be better sometimes? Just to end it.

I do. I think about that far more than I ought to. I sometimes think that when you die it's like you cross this threshold. You cross this door. You get out of here. *(Some time.)*

WILLIAM. There are other ways. Of getting out, you know. *(Chadwick nods.)*

When I'm twenty-one I'm going to inherit over half a million pounds. Did you know that? Did I ever tell you that?

CHADWICK. No.

WILLIAM. My dad made over twelve million pounds in the oil markets in Russia in the early nineties. He left half a million pounds of it to me in trust in his will. I inherit it when I'm twenty-one. I can do whatever I want with it.

I'm moving to New York. I'm going to go and live with Lilly. *(Chadwick looks at him.)*

We've planned it. Ask her if you don't believe me. We're going to get a warehouse loft conversion in the Lower East Side of Manhattan. I'm going to get a Lamborghini Esprit. Lilly'll probably get a haircut like Jennifer Lawrence or something like that. We'll drive around. That'll be better than being dead I think.

CHADWICK. Won't Nicholas mind?

WILLIAM. What?

CHADWICK. Won't Nicholas mind you living with Lilly?

WILLIAM. What has it got to do with him?

CHADWICK. She's going out with him.

WILLIAM. Who is?

CHADWICK. Lilly. She's been fucking him is what I heard.

WILLIAM. She's not.

CHADWICK. She has.

WILLIAM. Since when?

CHADWICK. Since about the first week she got here. *(Pause.)*

WILLIAM. Oh.

CHADWICK. Didn't you know?

WILLIAM. No. I didn't.

CHADWICK. Has it come as something of a blow?

WILLIAM. Well. I admit I am a little disappointed. *(Silence. Some time.)*

Can I stay at yours tonight?

CHADWICK. What?

WILLIAM. Can I stay at your house tonight?

CHADWICK. I don't know.

WILLIAM. What would your parents say if I just came round?

CHADWICK. I'm not sure they'd like it. With the exams next week and everything.

WILLIAM. They wouldn't do anything though, would they?

CHADWICK. I don't know.

WILLIAM. I could sleep on your floor. We could top and tail. We could get up in the middle of the night and make cheese on toast and eat it.

CHADWICK. No.

WILLIAM. What are you like at home?

CHADWICK. I don't know.

WILLIAM. Are you different?

CHADWICK. I don't think so.

WILLIAM. Do you behave differently than you do here? I bet you do. Do people like you there a bit more? I bet they do don't they? Why won't you let me stay then?

CHADWICK. It's not about letting you do anything. It's just not really my house.

WILLIAM. I could come round after the exams then. Couldn't I?

You know what it is that's wrong with your bone structure? I just figured it out. It's your nose. It's a little bit too high up your face I think. Isn't it? A bit too high up there?

I'm going to be fucking really fucking late now. I've got lessons all afternoon.

I have to say I feel like you've really let me down.

Scene 4

"The Woman Inside" by Cows.

It's 8:27 A.M. Monday, 10th November.

Bennett, Tanya, Nicholas, Cissy, William, and Lilly are in the common room.

BENNETT. What?

TANYA. A wasp!

CISSY. Where?

TANYA. There.

CISSY. Fuck.

NICHOLAS. That's not a wasp.

CISSY. Of course it's a wasp. Fuck.

TANYA. Get rid of it.

NICHOLAS. It's the middle of November. It's a fly.

TANYA. It's a wasp you fucking idiot. Open a window.

WILLIAM. I can't see it.

NICHOLAS. "Fucking idiot" that's a bit strong.

CISSY. There. My God it's by your head.

TANYA. It's gonna sting me.

CISSY. Get it. Kill it. Fuck!

WILLIAM. Don't kill it.

CISSY. What?

WILLIAM. Don't kill it.

TANYA. Has it gone yet?

WILLIAM. You mustn't kill it. It's a living creature.

CISSY. Are you being serious?

BENNETT. It's a fucking wasp.

NICHOLAS. Just open the window.

BENNETT. Wait.

TANYA. William please will you open the window.

BENNETT. Hold on. Watch.

CISSY. Bennett.

BENNETT. Trust me. Watch.

TANYA. William open the window.

BENNETT. No. Don't. William. Don't. Watch this. *(He moves to grab the wasp in his hand. He moves suddenly and with some elegance. He squeezes his fist closed. Opens it. He has caught and killed the dead wasp. The others look at him and at the wasp. He plucks it from his fist and holds it between two fingers.)*

CISSY. Oh my God.

NICHOLAS. How did you do that?

BENNETT. Magic. My dad taught me. You just have to watch the way they move.

TANYA. That's freaky. *(He looks at her.)*

BENNETT. You want to hold it?

TANYA. No thank you. It's really odd.

WILLIAM. I don't think it's odd. I think it's cruel. *(Bennett looks at the dead wasp. He gives it to William. William takes it. Looks at it. Puts it in his pocket.)*

CISSY. Cruel? How's it cruel? Wasps are vicious, pointless things.

NICHOLAS. It's pretty fucking impressive is what it is.

CISSY. Didn't it sting you? *(Chadwick enters.)*
BENNETT. Chadwick.

Stand there.

Now wait there.

Thanks.

No. They never do. Not if you're quick enough.
CHADWICK. Lloyd's had a heart attack. *(Everybody turns to look at him.)* Eliot just told me. He's in Stepping Hill. He nearly died. He didn't. They don't know how long he'll be in there.
BENNETT. Wow.
WILLIAM. What did you say?
CHADWICK. Late last night. Lloyd. He had a heart attack.
WILLIAM. A heart attack?
CHADWICK. It was quite severe. I think there were complications. Eliot said that somebody told him that he'd lost complete consciousness for a few seconds.
TANYA. Jesus.
WILLIAM. Lloyd?
CHADWICK. That's what I said.
WILLIAM. Is he dead?
CHADWICK. No. He's in hospital.
WILLIAM. But he died? For a bit?
CHADWICK. No. He lost consciousness that's different from dying.
BENNETT. You can't die for a bit.
WILLIAM. I saw him yesterday.
CHADWICK. Yes.
WILLIAM. I don't believe you.
CHADWICK. I'm not lying honestly. *(Pause.)*
CISSY. Fucking hell, eh?
TANYA. At his age. With that level of smoking. That's serious.

It's the History exam this afternoon as well.
WILLIAM. I'm going to go and see him. Does anybody want to come with me?

Does anybody want to come with me to see him?
TANYA. It's half eight, William.
WILLIAM. What?
TANYA. Maybe after school. We could go. We don't know what time visiting is.
WILLIAM. What?

41

TANYA. I'm not entirely sure he'll be able to take visitors for a couple of days. My granddad was like that. They kept him sleeping, mainly.

BENNETT. Did I tell you, you could fucking move.

Did I?

CHADWICK. No.

BENNETT. Then what the fuck are you moving for?

Today Chadwick, as a little tribute to a dying Lloyd, you are my doll. Do you understand me?

TANYA. Bennett.

BENNETT. What?

TANYA. Leave him alone. It's boring.

BENNETT. Boring? I'm not bored. Are you bored Chadwick? Are you bored Nicky?

TANYA. You're such a —

BENNETT. What?

What am I such a, Tanya? Come and tell me.

Ah. Fuck it. I'm playing. I'm playing. I'm being a prick.

Chadwick. Come in. Come in, lovely boy. I'm being an arsehole.

How are you today Chadders?

CHADWICK. I'm fine thank you.

BENNETT. Ready for your General Studies exam?

CHADWICK. Yes.

BENNETT. Me too, lovely, me too. It's my last one. I'm tempted to do it with my eyes closed.

That's awful fucking horrible news about Lloyd isn't it? I wonder what he looked like. I wonder if he stopped breathing. I wonder what colour he went. Have you ever seen anybody die, Chadders?

CHADWICK. No.

BENNETT. I heard you get an erection. Is he too old to get an erection do you think?

CISSY. Bennett.

BENNETT. I bet he's got a fucking huge cock. A really fucking big schlong, don't you think Chadders?

TANYA. You're sick.

BENNETT. Have you ever had an erection Chadwick?

TANYA. Don't.

BENNETT. What? I'm only asking. I'm only asking my mate Chadders.

Have you Chadwick? Have you ever had an erection Chadwick? Have you ever come?

CHADWICK. Yes.

BENNETT. How do you know?

CHADWICK. It's obvious isn't it? Don't you know that?

BENNETT. I can't imagine you coming. Do you wank all the time at home Chadwick? What do you think about when you're having a wank? Do you think about girls or boys?

CHADWICK. I think about girls. Don't you?

BENNETT. Your mum doesn't count Chadwick can I just say that?

Or do you think about fat little Tanya mainly? You're in there mate by the way. You should definitely ask her out. You'd make a lovely couple.

Have you ever had a girlfriend Chadwick? Chadwick answer my fucking question you uptight prick cunt.

CHADWICK. What?

BENNETT. Chadwick, have you ever had a girlfriend in your whole fucking life?

CHADWICK. No. I haven't. Not yet.

CISSY. Awww!

BENNETT. They will drop off eventually you know? They'll dry up and drop off. Like dead fruit.

CISSY. That's not true. Don't listen to him.

BENNETT. What do you think Nicky? Poor lamb's never been kissed. *(Nicholas doesn't answer.)*

CISSY. God. Can you imagine? Doing it with Chadwick. Sorry Chadwick. No offence or anything.

CHADWICK. No. None taken.

BENNETT. You should give him some tips Nicky. You get fucked all the time is what I heard.

NICHOLAS. Who told you that?

BENNETT. Everybody knows about that don't they Lilly? *(To Tanya.)* I can't believe you're being such a cocktease with him. It's fucking cruel if you ask me. *(To Nicholas.)* Haven't you got any mates who are interested in charity work?

NICHOLAS. No. Bennett. I haven't.

BENNETT. Couldn't you ask Copley for him?

CISSY. Have you seen her face?

BENNETT. Have you seen her cunt?

Her cunt is so fat.

TANYA. This is just —

BENNETT. Do you know what that means Chadwick? A fat cunt like that?

You don't do you?

Mind you, you wouldn't know what to do with it Chadwick, would you son? If she came up to you and bent over your desk in the middle of Physics to mark your work you wouldn't have a clue where to start.

CHADWICK. And you would?

BENNETT. What did you say?

CHADWICK. I said "And you would?" Know where to start. Bennett.

BENNETT. I don't believe you said that out loud.

CHADWICK. If she leant over your desk in the middle of Physics what are you saying you'd do?

BENNETT. I'd fuck her until she fucking screamed.

CHADWICK. Does that mean you're bisexual? *(A pause.)*

BENNETT. Tanya have you got some lipstick.

TANYA. What?

BENNETT. Have you? Have you got any lipstick Tanya?

CISSY. Bennett the bell's about to go. Everybody'll come out.

BENNETT. Can I ask you something Tanya old girl? Do you think I feel bad about myself because you keep on sticking up for him? Is that what you think? *(He goes to Chadwick. He grabs a fistful of his hair, really tightly.)*

Tanya. Take your lipstick out or I'll properly hurt him.

There.

Now Chadwick come over to Tanya. And she'll put some lipstick on for you.

TANYA. What?

BENNETT. Come on Tanya.

CISSY. Oh my God.

BENNETT. Chadwick come to Tanya. Purse your lips.

Tanya.

(He spits in her face.)

Do it.

Now.

Thank you.

CHADWICK. It's nice.

CISSY. What?

CHADWICK. I like it. It smells nice.

BENNETT. You look so fucking gay Chadwick you make me want to do a piss.

Kiss him.

CISSY. What?

BENNETT. Kiss him. For me. *(She looks at Bennett. She goes to Chadwick. She kisses him with a real sexuality.)* What are you doing William?

WILLIAM. Just having a bit of a dance.

BENNETT. *(Watches Cissy kiss Chadwick.)* Hey Chadwick. That's my girlfriend. *(Chadwick and Cissy stop kissing.)* What the fuck are you doing kissing my fucking girlfriend.

CHADWICK. You told me to.

CISSY. He tasted like crisps.

BENNETT. Right in front of me.

CHADWICK. You told me to. Bennett. I didn't want to.

BENNETT. You didn't want to? What are you saying? What are you saying about Cissy, Chadwick? Are you calling her? First you snog her right in front of me and then you go and call her like that. I should cut your face off for that. I should cut your ears off. I should cut your needle dick off. You fucking pervert fuckhead cunt.

WILLIAM. Stop it Bennett.

BENNETT. What?

WILLIAM. Stop it.

Just leave him alone.

BENNETT. Are you actually talking to *me* now?

WILLIAM. You're a complete fucking prick. Leave him alone.

BENNETT. Listen to him.

WILLIAM. I mean it Bennett. Leave him alone. Now.

BENNETT. Listen to the brother-fucker over here.

WILLIAM. What did you say?

BENNETT. Oh. I think you heard me William didn't you?

WILLIAM. Come here. Come here and say that.

BENNETT. I said "Listen to the brother-fucker over here." I was talking about you. I was referring to your dead brother.

WILLIAM. I'll kill you for that.

LILLY. William calm down. He was winding you up. *(The bell goes. They go to move.)*

WILLIAM. Where are you all fucking going. Stay there. Stay there Bennett. I'm not scared of you. I'm not scared of anybody. You want to know how hard I am?

LILLY. William. It's registration.

WILLIAM. Come on Bennet. You cunt. You fuckhead. Come on then. Anytime. You and me. Outside. Now.

BENNETT. Have you heard him? He's talking like a character from a film.

WILLIAM. I could beat you in a fight really easily.

BENNETT. I'm sure you could.

WILLIAM. I tell you. One day, soon, you are going to get the surprise of your life. *(To Chadwick.)* Don't listen to him. He's worth nothing. He's just a big empty vacuous awful space.

CHADWICK. I don't mind.

BENNETT. Don't you?

CHADWICK. I don't worry about you lot anymore.

BENNETT. Well. That's big of you.

CHADWICK. Human beings are pathetic. Everything human beings do finishes up bad in the end. Everything good human beings ever make is built on something monstrous. Nothing lasts. We certainly won't. We could have made something really extraordinary and we won't. We've been around one hundred thousand years. We'll have died out before the next two hundred. You know what we've got to look forward to? You know what will define the next two hundred years? Religions will become brutalised; crime rates will become hysterical; everybody will become addicted to internet sex; suicide will become fashionable; there'll be famine; there'll be floods; there'll be epidemics in the major cities of the Western World. Our education systems will become battered. Our health services unsustainable; our police forces unmanageable; our governments corrupt. There'll be open brutality in the streets; there'll be nuclear war; massive depletion of resources on every level; insanely increasing third-world population. It's happening already. It's happening now. Thousands die every summer from floods in the Indian monsoon season. Africans from Senegal wash up on the beaches of the Mediterranean and get looked after by guilty liberal holiday makers. Somalians wait in hostels in Malta or prison islands north of Australia. Hundreds die of heat or fire every year in Paris. Or California. Or Athens. The oceans will rise. The cities will flood. The power stations will flood. Airports will flood. Species will vanish forever. Including ours. So if you think I'm worried by you calling me names Bennett you little, little boy you are fucking kidding yourself.

BENNETT. Blimey.

That's a bit bleak Chadwick.

CHADWICK. Just because something's bleak doesn't mean it's not true.

CISSY. I don't believe that.

CHADWICK. You should do.

CISSY. We can educate each other.

CHADWICK. We don't.

CISSY. We can change things.

CHADWICK. We can't.

CISSY. We can. There's science. There's technology.

CHADWICK. It won't help now.

CISSY. People have always said the world's going to end.

CHADWICK. They were wrong. I'm really fucking not.

I was right about your lipstick too Tanya. It does taste nice. *(He licks his own lips. Leaves.)*

BENNETT. Ah! First period! Once more into the breach. What time's the exam?

10 o'clock isn't it? Lovely. That was fun that William. I rather enjoyed myself. Same time tomorrow old bean?

Until the exam hall, lovelies. Don't be late. *(He leaves.)*

CISSY. We've got English. *(No response …)*

We'll be late. *(No response …)*

At least he'll notice you.

TANYA. Yeah. *(Tanya leaves. Cissy stands for a moment. She follows.)*

NICHOLAS. Are you all right?

WILLIAM. Am I what?

NICHOLAS. I was asking if you were OK.

WILLIAM. Do I not look it?

LILLY. It's good that you stood up to him.

WILLIAM. Are you both free now?

LILLY. Until the exam.

WILLIAM. Well. You'll like that.

NICHOLAS. I can't believe they make us do a lesson. For one period —

WILLIAM. Have they turned the heating off in here?

NICHOLAS. No. I'm really warm.

LILLY. I'm boiling. *(William looks at her.)*

WILLIAM. I feel a little bit let down.

LILLY. What by William?

WILLIAM. It's hard because there are some things that have happened that are entirely my fault.

LILLY. What like?

WILLIAM. You know what like.

LILLY. I don't.

WILLIAM. All of you talk about it all the time.

I'm not that naïve. I know I might look it. I know I might look like oh William. William Billiam. William Tell. William the Thick. William the Great. Do you think I'm William Shakespeare? *(They look at him.)* Because I might be. It's entirely possible. Look at the news!

NICHOLAS. What?

WILLIAM. A hundred and ninety people were killed yesterday in a plane crash in Brazil. Why do you think that happened?

LILLY. It skidded. On the runway. The runway was wet.

WILLIAM. Oh right. Yeah.

NICHOLAS. That's true.

WILLIAM. That's what they tell you is true.

NICHOLAS. Are you saying you caused the plane crash William?

WILLIAM. Wouldn't you like to know?

I bet you really —

How long have you been going out you two?

NICHOLAS. William.

WILLIAM. Why the fuck won't anybody come with me to Lloyd's funeral for fucksake!

LILLY. He's not dead. He didn't die. Chadwick said —

WILLIAM. They should close the whole school is what they fucking well should do.

How many times have you fucked her Nicholas?

NICHOLAS. William, shut up.

WILLIAM. Or what? Is his cock really huge?

LILLY. Be quiet. You're making a fool of yourself.

WILLIAM. What?

What?

Have I said something really embarrassing?

I'm sorry.

God.

I'm really sorry. I didn't even hear myself speak.

Come here. Come here Lilly. My best friend.

LILLY. William get off.

WILLIAM. *(Kisses the side of her head.)* I could eat you. I'd better go now.

LILLY. William, where are you going?

WILLIAM. I'm going to go and see Lloyd. Get a bit of conversation. Bit of stimulation. You know what I mean?

LILLY. You've got your exams.

WILLIAM. I've got what?

LILLY. You've got the General Studies exam. You've got History this afternoon. *(William looks at her briefly, slightly confused by what she's talking about. Then he leaves. They watch him go. They look at each other.)*

NICHOLAS. Are you OK?

LILLY. I think so. Are you?

NICHOLAS. Yes. *(They hold each other's gaze for a while.)*

Scene 5

"Fell in Love with a Girl" by the White Stripes.

It's 4:38 P.M. Monday, 10th November.

LILLY. What?

What?

Aren't you going to talk to me?

Are you just going to look at me, William because it's creeping me out a bit?

Why are all the windows open? Did you open them?

What did you want? Where have you been all day?

Look. I got your text. You asked me to come here so I came.

It's dark. I'm going to go home unless you speak to me. I mean it.

WILLIAM. Mr. Lloyd died. This morning. When we were in here.

I went up to the hospital after I left you and Nicholas. I was too late. I tried to get you all to come earlier. You all stopped me.

It was a horrible place.

He's the second person I ever met who's died now. How many people do you know who've died?

I was meant to have exams wasn't I? I got lost coming home. I was wandering around.

Have I missed them? My exams? Did I miss History? *(Lilly nods.)*

While I was wandering about I realised something about you. I figured out what you are. In real life. It came to me. Like an epiphany.

LILLY. What are you talking about?

WILLIAM. You're a robot aren't you?

LILLY. What?

WILLIAM. Where did they make you? What laboratory did they make you in?

When I asked you out, were you already going out with Nicholas?

You were, weren't you? Why didn't you tell me? Why didn't you say anything about it?

Can you hear that?

LILLY. What?

WILLIAM. That banging.

LILLY. No.

WILLIAM. Are you lying?

LILLY. I didn't know what to say. I really liked you. I really like you. I didn't want to let you down.

WILLIAM. Good answer. I bought you a present when I was out and about. It's a very early Christmas present.

LILLY. Fucking hell.

WILLIAM. "Fucking hell." If my mum could hear you swearing.

LILLY. You can't give me this.

WILLIAM. "You can't give me this." Yes I can. I just did. I got one too. Look, I downloaded some songs for you.

LILLY. William there's three hundred songs on here.

WILLIAM. "William there's three hundred songs on here." Ha!

LILLY. Did you buy all these?

WILLIAM. "Did you buy all these?"

LILLY. I thought you said your mum was dead.

WILLIAM. My step-mum.

Don't.

LILLY. What?

WILLIAM. Look at me like that. You look exactly like her. I really hate it.

Will you do me a favour? In return for my present?

LILLY. It depends what it is.

WILLIAM. Will you stop burning yourself? Because I don't think it's very good for you. I think you'd be better off stopping.

Will you Lilly? Do you promise? *(A long pause.)*

LILLY. I'll try.

WILLIAM. Try really hard.

LILLY. William are you all right?

WILLIAM. I'm just a bit.

LILLY. What?

WILLIAM. I can't think of the word.

LILLY. For what?

WILLIAM. When you haven't slept enough?

LILLY. Tired?

WILLIAM. Yes. I'm a bit tired.

LILLY. You couldn't remember the word "tired."

WILLIAM. Some of the things you told me weren't true.

LILLY. What things?

WILLIAM. You know what things. There's a lot about you which is a lie. The way you tie your tie is a lie. You're lying with the way you tie your fucking tie.

LILLY. This is exhausting me.

WILLIAM. Yeah.

LILLY. I'm going home.

WILLIAM. Don't.

LILLY. Why shouldn't I?

WILLIAM. I'm scared of what I might do if you leave. *(She looks at him.)*

LILLY. Yeah.

We all get scared William.

Sometimes the world is a bit unnerving. Some people do awful things but, and you need to listen to this William, seriously, most of the time the world is all right. You need to get that into your head and stop moping about.

WILLIAM. Moping? Is that what you think I'm doing?

LILLY. Most people are all right.

WILLIAM. They're not.

LILLY. They're funny. They chat a bit. They tell jokes. They're kind. They're all right.

WILLIAM. You so should have gone to another school.

LILLY. When I was twelve —

WILLIAM. When you were what?

LILLY. Listen to me. I'm trying to tell you something. When I was twelve I used to get headaches.

WILLIAM. What are you talking about?

LILLY. They were properly fierce. It used to feel as though the front of my head was being carved in two. They could really bring tears to my eyes. I didn't tell my mum about them for weeks —

WILLIAM. Why are you telling me this?

LILLY. But after about two weeks I did.

WILLIAM. I think you've gone a bit mad.

LILLY. I told her. She took me to the doctor and the doctor gave me some aspirin and told me to drink more water and get some more fresh air and to eat less sugar and so I did and the headaches went away.

WILLIAM. I'm not talking about headaches. This is more than a headache.

LILLY. Maybe you should tell somebody.

WILLIAM. Are you trying to inspire me? With your little tiny story? You want to inspire me? Take your top off. That'll inspire me. Let me see your tits. That'd be a massive inspiration I think. That'd really cheer me up Lilly. Honestly.

LILLY. I'm sorry I didn't want to go out with you. I wanted to go out with Nicholas instead.

I really love him.

But I always thought you'd be my mate. And I would still really like to be in spite of everything. Because actually I think you're not that well and I'm worried about you and I want to get you some help.

WILLIAM. Ha!

LILLY. What?

WILLIAM. Can I ask you this: When you have sex with him, with Nicholas, does it hurt?

Does it?

Please tell me.

LILLY. No.

WILLIAM. Doesn't it?

LILLY. No.

WILLIAM. What's it like?

LILLY. It's lovely.

WILLIAM. Right. That's good. That's good for you. I don't like him. Personally. I think he's a fraud. I think he's a liar. I think he's made of lies and shit. But that's just my opinion.

LILLY. He isn't.

WILLIAM. I am completely entitled to my own opinion. Don't you dare try to tell me that I'm not because I fucking am. *(Some time.)*

LILLY. Nicholas told me that you were lying about your parents.

Why did you lie about your parents William?

WILLIAM. I didn't. I wasn't. I didn't lie.

LILLY. He told me your parents are still alive but that you had a brother and it was your brother who died when he was a baby.

WILLIAM. Lies, damn lies and statistics.

LILLY. Is that true about your brother?

WILLIAM. Can you hear it?

LILLY. What?

WILLIAM. I can hear it again. That banging.

LILLY. I can't hear it at all.

WILLIAM. There was a boy killed himself here once. When it was a boy's school. He climbed onto the roof of the quad. Jumped off. This was back in the seventies. Maybe it's him.

Were there a lot of gypsies in Cambridge?

LILLY. What?

WILLIAM. We should sort them out, us two, I reckon. Go on a march.

LILLY. Sort who out?

WILLIAM. I know we could. When two people love each other as much as we do then I think they can do anything.

LILLY. I don't love you.

WILLIAM. You must do.

LILLY. I don't William. *(A long pause. Longer than you think you can get away with. William turns the lights off. He stands still for a long time.)* Can you turn the light back on please William?

WILLIAM. I'm sorry. Did you say something?

LILLY. You're starting to —

WILLIAM. I don't blame you. By the way. I'm rubbish me. I'm a waste of time. I'm not even worth the space I take up. I'm not even worth the paper I'm written on. I've got no friends. I've got no imagination. I've got no ideas.

LILLY. Stop it.

WILLIAM. I hate my shoes. I hate my house. I hate this school. I hate my hair. Can I have a haircut?

LILLY. What?

WILLIAM. Will you give me a haircut please? A better one. One that makes me look less of a fucking spastic —

LILLY. Don't say that.

WILLIAM. — than this haircut makes me look.

LILLY. I hate that word.

WILLIAM. Cut my hair.

LILLY. With what?

WILLIAM. I don't care. Your hands. Your ruler. Pull it out.
I'm just. I want it to stop.
You know when I'm with you?

LILLY. I've only known you a month.

WILLIAM. I feel like I'm earthed. Here. *(He touches the side of her head with the palm of his hand. Nothing apparently happens or changes.)*
And watch what happens if I let go. *(He lets go.)*
See? *(Nothing apparently happens or changes. He smiles for a while. He stops smiling quite suddenly.)*
Who are you?

LILLY. What?

WILLIAM. I don't know who you are.

LILLY. —

WILLIAM. Can I tell you something?

LILLY. What?

WILLIAM. Do you want a word of advice? A word to the wise?

LILLY. —

WILLIAM. Tomorrow.

LILLY. What?

WILLIAM. Don't come into school.

Scene 6

"Touch Me I'm Sick" by Mudhoney.

It's 8:57 A.M. Tuesday, 11th November.

The stage remains empty for a while. Bennett enters. Then Nicholas.

BENNETT. They've marked the exams. *(Nicholas looks at him for a while.)*
NICHOLAS. What?
BENNETT. I just saw Gilchrist. She said she'll give us our results later.
NICHOLAS. Fuck.
BENNETT. Yeah. She had a remarkable look on her face. It was like a combination of glee and fury.
I absolutely know that I have really properly fucked them all up.
My parents will go fucking mental.
NICHOLAS. Yeah.
BENNETT. They'll drag out the same old speeches. About the fees. "Do you know what we have to do to get the money to send you to that place? Do you have the slightest idea how much it costs every year?"
I don't actually. Do you?
NICHOLAS. Have you seen Lilly?
BENNETT. I've not seen anybody all morning. Maybe they're all hiding. Maybe they all know something we don't.
Aren't you worried at all about your results?
NICHOLAS. Too late to change anything now.
BENNETT. Well that's very fucking mature I have to say. *(He lights a cigarette. He looks at Nicholas.)* How are things going with her? With Lilly?
NICHOLAS. They're all right, thank you.
BENNETT. She's lovely.
NICHOLAS. Yes. She is.

BENNETT. She's surprisingly smart. I like her 'cause she's rock hard. She's very lucky.

Did you hear that Tanya's dad came up to the school?

NICHOLAS. Lilly mentioned that she'd seen him.

BENNETT. Yesterday lunchtime he came and spoke to Edwards. She must have rang him during the day. The fat bitch. He kept me here till half past six last night. Bastard. He was probably marking our exams while I was sat there doing fucking lines.

NICHOLAS. You shouldn't have spat at her. *(Bennett looks at Nicholas for a beat.)*

BENNETT. No. I shouldn't have done.

It was stupid. I just really wanted to. I wanted to try it out. I wanted to know what it would feel like.

Do you ever get things like that?

NICHOLAS. I'm not sure.

BENNETT. Have you ever wanted to set fire to things?

NICHOLAS. Nothing serious. Maybe the occasional dustbin.

BENNETT. Have you ever wanted to blow something up.

NICHOLAS. Fuck yeah. Who hasn't?

BENNETT. Have you ever wanted to kiss a boy?

NICHOLAS. No.

BENNETT. Never?

NICHOLAS. No.

BENNETT. Liar.

NICHOLAS. I'm not lying.

BENNETT. I wanted to kiss Thom Yorke once.

NICHOLAS. Yeah?

BENNETT. And David Bowie. *(Nicholas looks at him for a beat. Smiles at him. Pause.)*

NICHOLAS. I was so hungover this morning I couldn't believe it.

BENNETT. Where were you last night?

NICHOLAS. I went out with my brother. He's come home for Christmas.

BENNETT. Already? Fucking students. How is he?

NICHOLAS. He's really well. Mum and Dad are happy to see him.

BENNETT. How's Durham?

NICHOLAS. He loves it, I think.

BENNETT. That's good. Are you all going away for Christmas or something?

NICHOLAS. I don't think so.

BENNETT. We're going to fucking Reykjavík of all places. *(Nicholas looks at him. Smiles.)*

NICHOLAS. I shouldn't have been drinking. I'm on painkillers for my ankle. I feel fucking shit now.

BENNETT. What happened to your ankle?

NICHOLAS. I twisted it. Playing rugby.

BENNETT. When was this?

NICHOLAS. Last week.

BENNETT. You never told me this. *(Nicholas looks at him.)*
Can I see it? *(Nicholas shows him his ankle.)*
It looks red, Nicholas.

NICHOLAS. Yeah. You should have seen it last week. *(Bennett touches it. He winces as he touches it, as though feeling Nicholas's pain.)*
It's all right. It doesn't really hurt anymore. *(Cissy enters.)*

CISSY. Don't tell my mum. Don't tell my mum. Don't tell my mum. Don't tell my mum.

NICHOLAS. Don't tell your mum what?

CISSY. I just saw Anderson. I got a B for English.

BENNETT. Fucking hell.

CISSY. I know.

NICHOLAS. A B's not bad.

CISSY. Are you being serious?

NICHOLAS. A B's good I think.

CISSY. If she finds out she'll kill me.

NICHOLAS. Cissy, I think you're exaggerating.

BENNETT. You don't know her mother.

CISSY. How can I stop her from finding out?

NICHOLAS. Don't tell her.

CISSY. She'll get the report.

BENNETT. Hide it. Burn it.

CISSY. Don't be fucking stupid Bennett. She knows there'll be a report. It's the end of the term. There's always a report.

BENNETT. Tipp-Ex over it.

CISSY. Oh you're *so* not helping. *(Tanya enters.)*

TANYA. What is the matter with you?

CISSY. I got my English results.

TANYA. Already?

BENNETT. She got a B.

TANYA. Ouch! Have you ever got a B in anything before?

NICHOLAS. She's worried her mother's going to kill her.

TANYA. Yeah. She will.

CISSY. If I fuck up —

BENNETT. You already have sweetheart.

CISSY. No, properly. If I properly fuck up. If I don't get the grades I need for my place in the summer, not in the mocks, in the real exams, then I'll go —

I don't know what I'll do.

TANYA. You won't. Fuck up. You're being really stupid. These are just mocks.

CISSY. I'll never get out of Stockport. I'll never leave. I'll be stuck here forever. There's a whole world out there and I'll never see it once, not ever. All these things I want to do, I won't be able to do them.

TANYA. You keep going on about that. *(Cissy looks at her.)*

It's not about Stockport, Cissy. It's about you. You were made here. You keep trying to pretend that you weren't. It's ridiculous. *(The two girls look at each other.)*

CISSY. I don't know what to say.

And I don't know what you're laughing at.

BENNETT. What?

CISSY. You're meant to be my boyfriend.

BENNETT. Oh, come on!

CISSY. You're meant to stick up for me.

BENNETT. It was funny. She was being funny.

CISSY. All you ever do is laugh at me.

BENNETT. Well. Can you blame me?

CISSY. What?

BENNETT. You *are* ridiculous. For somebody so clever you're unbelievably fucking stupid. How could I fail to laugh at you?

Isn't she? Isn't she Nicky? *(Chadwick enters.)*

Chadwick, isn't Cissy fucking ridiculous?

CHADWICK. I don't think so. She's always seemed rather intelligent to me.

BENNETT. I'm not denying that. I'm not talking about her intelligence for fucksake. *(William enters.)*

William. Answer me this. Why is it that every single person in this school judges everybody else by the level of their intelligence? Not by their wit. Not by their appearance. Not by their dress sense. Not by their taste in music. By how many A-stars they got at GCSE.

WILLIAM. *(Pulls a gun out of the inside pocket of his blazer.)* I've no

58

idea. *(He shoots his gun at the lights in the common room. He smashes the bulbs. The room darkens.)*

It works then.

I did warn you Bennett. Don't say I didn't warn you because I really fucking did. *(He points his gun at Bennett.)*

BENNETT. What? What the fuck? No. No. God. Please. Don't. *(Bennett cowers away from him. Wherever he goes to William follows him with his gun.)*

NICHOLAS. William. *(William turns to look at him. Points the gun at him when he does.)*

WILLIAM. Yeah. What?

NICHOLAS. Don't.

WILLIAM. Don't what? *(Tanya has started crying. Cissy moves to the door.)*

Don't. Cissy. Fucking just don't.

NICHOLAS. William. People will come.

WILLIAM. What?

NICHOLAS. People will have heard the gunshot. They'll be here any second.

WILLIAM. Do you think so?

I can't hear anybody coming. Can you hear anybody? *(They listen.)*

NICHOLAS. Put the gun down before anybody gets hurt.

WILLIAM. Don't be fucking stupid.

It feels funny. It's a lot lighter than I thought it would be. It's a lot easier to aim.

Hey Bennett. Hey Bennett. Get up. Bennett. Stop fucking crying and fucking listen to me.

You know when you spat at Tanya, what was it like?

What did it feel like?

What was it like for you Tanya?

TANYA. William, stop it.

WILLIAM. I heard you got a detention. Shit.

Did your parents find out?

Bennett. Did your parents find out?

Did your parents find out about your detention Bennett?

BENNETT. No.

WILLIAM. Didn't they?

How come? What did you tell them? What did you tell them Bennett?

BENNETT. I told them I was at football practise.

WILLIAM. Ha! Did you? How did you think of that? That's fucking brilliant. That's fucking genius is what that is.

Can I tell you something Bennett?

No other animal in the world polices its behaviour via a third person. Did you know that?

BENNETT. Did I know what?

WILLIAM. If a monkey steals another monkey's nuts he doesn't go and get a third monkey to sort him out. If a cat shits on another cat's tree that cat doesn't go and tell a big huge third cat and get him to sort the first cat out. Does he? No. Of course he doesn't. Only human beings do that. I hate it. You spat at Tanya. Tanya should have stabbed you or something. She didn't. She rang home and told her dad. It's pathetic. As far as I'm concerned that means you're free to do whatever you want with her. Batter her. Shoot her. Rape her. She's the only one who should be able to stop you.

Don't you think?

Don't you think Bennett?

Everybody's being really fucking quiet today.

Don't you think, Nicholas, shouldn't Bennett be allowed to rape Tanya now?

NICHOLAS. No.

WILLIAM. What?

NICHOLAS. I said no. He shouldn't. That's horrible. That's a crazy idea.

WILLIAM. What did you say? *(He looks at him for a long time.)*

NICHOLAS. I said that's a crazy idea.

WILLIAM. Don't say that.

NICHOLAS. We can't operate like —

BENNETT. Don't, Nicholas.

NICHOLAS. We can't control a community —

BENNETT. Nicholas be quiet for God's sake.

WILLIAM. Ah! That's quite sweet. He's protecting you look.

I don't want to talk about this any more.

(He shoots Bennett twice. He dies. Cissy screams. She tries to stop herself. There is some quietness. Some stillness for a while.)

Can you smell burning?

Something's burning. Can you smell?

NICHOLAS. No.

WILLIAM. Here. Nicholas.

NICHOLAS. What?

WILLIAM. Watch this. *(He shoots Cissy. She dies.)*

NICHOLAS. William! *(Tanya is crying. Chadwick is crying.)*

WILLIAM. Did you say something?

CHADWICK. Me?

WILLIAM. Yeah.

CHADWICK. No.

WILLIAM. I thought you said something.

CHADWICK. I didn't.

WILLIAM. I thought somebody said something. Just now. About — Did you say something about a fire?

CHADWICK. No.

WILLIAM. You did. I heard you.

CHADWICK. I didn't William.

WILLIAM. It's probably just me. Is it just me? Am I the only one who heard him talking about the fire?

This happens to me all the time. *(Points his gun at Nicholas.)*

You know when you're thinking?

NICHOLAS. Thinking? Yes. I know when I'm thinking —

WILLIAM. When you're thinking yeah and in order to like make a decision yes? Sometimes you have to weigh one side up against the other and you need to have a jolly good debate in your head about what is the right thing to do and what is the wrong thing to do, yes? And sometimes when you're doing this each side kind of has a voice in your head. You know that?

NICHOLAS. I think so, William.

WILLIAM. Sometimes when I do that — The voices sound like they're coming from over there. Or over there. Or over there. Sometimes. Not often. That sounded as though it was coming from Chadwick. How very embarrassing. I am sorry.

NICHOLAS. Don't be.

WILLIAM. I am. I will be. Because I am. You can't exactly choose these things can you?

Can you hear anybody coming? *(They listen.)*

Told you. *(He turns away from Chadwick. Without William noticing, Chadwick takes the opportunity to turn and run through the classroom door. William notices him too late. He points his gun. He puts it down again. He laughs a little.)*

He got away! *(He turns and shoots Nicholas. Nicholas dies. He looks around at what he's done. There's some time. He looks at Tanya.*

She's crying her heart out.)

Did you hear about Lilly?

TANYA. What about her.

WILLIAM. She's dead.

TANYA. Dead?

WILLIAM. Not literally. She's just in a bit of trouble.

TANYA. Why?

WILLIAM. She did something.

TANYA. What?

WILLIAM. Something really bad.

TANYA. What did she do?

WILLIAM. What's wrong?

TANYA. Nothing.

WILLIAM. You're crying.

TANYA. Yeah.

WILLIAM. You're so lovely. Don't cry. Here. *(Smiles. Goes to hug her. She is terrified. He hugs her. Lets go. Sits down on a table. A long pause.)*

Dear God. Please — Dear God … Are you there? Dear God please look after little baby Alistair and Mum and Dad and — *(He breaks into uncontrollable giggles.)*

I always find it hard to keep a straight face. *(He goes to shoot himself. He holds his gun in his mouth. After a short while he retracts it.)*

I'm sorry. I really need a piss. Should I do it on the floor? Should I do it in my trousers, Tanya? If I do it in my trousers will you tell?

TANYA. No.

WILLIAM. Do you think it'd be all right? *(She nods. He pisses in his trousers, down his trouser leg, onto the floor of the common room.)*

My God. The relief. *(He breaks into an enormous smile.)*

Scene 7

"Desperate Man Blues" by Daniel Johnston.

It's 11:59 A.M. December 24th.

William Carlisle and Dr Richard Harvey are in a clinical examination room of Suttons Manor medium-security hospital.

The walls of the room are white. It is very brightly lit.

Dr Harvey wears an immaculately smart brown suit. William wears joggers and a sweatshirt.

William is completing a questionnaire. He has to tick boxes in answers to questions. The questionnaire is twenty-five pages long.

There is some time before Dr Harvey speaks.

HARVEY. Would you like to rest?
WILLIAM. No.
HARVEY. You can do.
WILLIAM. I don't want to. *(He answers another question.)*
    I like this kind of test.
    It's quite funny.
    Have you done it?
    Did you make these questions up?
HARVEY. With a colleague.
WILLIAM. How many are there in total?
HARVEY. One thousand eight hundred.
WILLIAM. *(Looks at him. Smiles.)* Great.
    It's like doing a comprehension test. A bit.
    Doing a comprehension test on your brain.
    "Do you feel confident in clothes shops?"
    "Do you feel confident in music shops?"
    "Do you feel confident in cafés?"

"Do you feel confident in libraries?"

"Do you feel confident in supermarkets?"

"Do you feel confident at football matches?"

"Do you feel confident in school classrooms?"

"Do you feel confident in furniture shops?"

"Do you feel confident in licensed adult shops?" Is that sex shops?

HARVEY. That's right.

WILLIAM. "Do you feel confident in greengrocers?"

"Do you feel confident in newsagents?"

"Do you feel confident in playgrounds?"

"Do you feel confident in estate agents?" *(He fills in more of the forms. Dr. Harvey watches him. He writes a little as William is talking. After a while William puts his pen down.)*

I'm not allowed a cigarette am I?

HARVEY. I'm afraid not.

WILLIAM. I could just have a cheeky one. *(Harvey smiles.)*

You laugh but I'm being serious.

I'm getting a bit tired now. You shouldn't have put the idea in my head.

It's the Droperidol. The Haloperidol. *(William answers a question. He looks up again.)*

Is it Christmas yet?

HARVEY. Tomorrow.

WILLIAM. It's Christmas Eve?

HARVEY. That's right.

WILLIAM. *(Thinks.)* Do you know who I am?

HARVEY. Sorry?

WILLIAM. I never know with you lot if they tell you who I am before I meet you or if they try and keep it neutral.

HARVEY. I'm not sure if I know what you mean.

WILLIAM. Did they tell you what I did?

That means they did, didn't they?

What's your name?

HARVEY. Harvey. Dr Harvey.

WILLIAM. What's your first name? That's not Harvey too is it? Harvey Harvey? Dr Harvey Harvey?

HARVEY. No. My first name's Richard.

WILLIAM. Happy Christmas Richard.

HARVEY. Happy Christmas. *(They smile at each other.)*

WILLIAM. Can I ask you something: When you found out that you were coming to meet me, did you get a bit excited?

HARVEY. Excited?

WILLIAM. It's always exciting meeting celebrities, isn't it?

You must have wondered what I'd be like, did you?

HARVEY. I've been doing this job long enough to know that you can never really predict what a patient is going to be like, or how they're going to behave. Regardless of how much of their record you've had access to.

WILLIAM. Or what you've read about them in newspapers.

HARVEY. I honestly don't read newspapers.

WILLIAM. But you know who I am, don't you? You know what I did? Do you know what I did? Richard do you know what I did?

HARVEY. Yeah. Yes I do.

WILLIAM. Does it freak you out a bit being in here with me?

HARVEY. No.

WILLIAM. Have you got a panic button?

HARVEY. Yes I do.

WILLIAM. Is it underneath your desk?

Have you got any children? Have you Richard?

HARVEY. I've a daughter.

WILLIAM. How old is she?

HARVEY. She's seventeen.

WILLIAM. My age.

Does it make you sick what I did?

Does it make you sick what I did?

HARVEY. No.

WILLIAM. You're lying. I can tell by the way you look to the left. When people look to the right they're thinking. When they look to the left they're lying.

Can I have a glass of water please?

HARVEY. Certainly. *(He stands to leave.)*

WILLIAM. I'll just wait here. *(Dr Harvey enjoys the joke. He exits. Some time. Nicholas Chatman enters. He sits opposite William. William almost laughs. He stares at him.)*

Nicholas? Nicky? *(He goes to touch his face.)*

Are you OK? Are you dead?

Does it hurt?

Did I hurt you?

I'm — *(Nicholas stands suddenly. He exits as though he'd forgotten*

65

something and has to rush to get it. William is left on his own. He tries to gather himself. He starts to cry a little bit. He stops himself and rubs his eyes dry furiously. Dr Harvey returns with a glass of water and three cigarettes and a box of three matches.)

HARVEY. Sorry the cooler was empty. I had to go up to the second floor.

WILLIAM. Thank you. *(Drinks.)*

HARVEY. I got you these. Here. *(He gives William the cigarettes. William smiles broadly.)*

WILLIAM. Fucking hell. Thank you. *(He takes a cigarette and opens the matches. Notices there are only three. Laughs once. Takes one. Strikes it. Lights his cigarette. Smiles broadly.)*

That tastes lovely.

(He smokes.)

See the main question people have been asking me is why I did it? Why do people keep asking me that?

HARVEY. I think people are concerned about you.

WILLIAM. "Why did you do it William?" "What did you do it for?" "Why did you do that?" "Why did you do this?" *(He answers some more questions. As he answers the questions he talks. His ticking becomes more frantic. By the end of his speech he is almost cutting into the paper with his pen. Dr Harvey takes a few notes.)*

I don't know. I don't care. It's a pointless question. It's a stupid question. It's a boring question. Next question please. Next question please. Next question please. Was it because of my mum? No. Was it because of my dad? No. Was it because of my brother? No. Was it because of my school? No. Was it because of the teachers? No. Was it because of Lilly? No. Was it the music I was listening to? No. Was it the films I saw? No. Was it the books that I read? No. Was it the things I saw on the internet? No. *(He scribbles onto the paper. Puts his pen down.)*

I did it because I could. *(He smokes.)*

There was a bullet left in the gun. I was going to shoot myself. I actually put the gun to my mouth. Did you hear about that? Tanya was there, she could tell you this.

Is she all right? Tanya?

HARVEY. She's recovering. She and Chadwick Meade both hope to go back to school at the start of next term. *(William thinks about this.)*

WILLIAM. When you went to get the water were you watching me? You don't need to answer that by the way. *(Dr Harvey smiles.)*

Will you be coming back after today?

HARVEY. We don't know yet. I need to complete my report by the end of next week. *(William nods.)*

WILLIAM. What are you going to say about me in your report?

HARVEY. I don't quite know yet.

WILLIAM. And after you they'll probably send somebody else.

HARVEY. That hasn't been decided.

WILLIAM. They probably will. They send new people all the time.

I should go and get a job. Do something proper. Do something worthwhile I think. Don't you think?

HARVEY. In time.

WILLIAM. No. Not in time. Now.

Look. I'm not an — I'm not. I'm not an idiot. I know that something's going on. I know something's a bit wrong.

I want to be an architect. Build buildings way up as high as I can get them to go. Get some children. Just be normal. Go to hospital one day and get my head sorted out. Buy a small house. Not spend too much money. *(He answers some more questions. Then stops. He looks up. He looks at Dr Harvey. Light falls suddenly.)*

End of Play

PROPERTY LIST

Bic lighter
Apple
Chip sandwich
Carrots
Mineral water bottle with Campari and grapefruit juice
Protein drink
Wallet
£20
Cell phone
Dead wasp
MP3 player
Lipstick
Cigarettes
Gun
Long questionnaire
Pen
Glass of water
Box of matches

SOUND EFFECTS

Passing train
Wasp buzzing
Bell
Gunshots

NEW PLAYS

★ **MOTHERS AND SONS by Terrence McNally.** At turns funny and powerful, MOTHERS AND SONS portrays a woman who pays an unexpected visit to the New York apartment of her late son's partner, who is now married to another man and has a young son. Challenged to face how society has changed around her, generations collide as she revisits the past and begins to see the life her son might have led. "A resonant elegy for a ravaged generation." –NY Times. "A moving reflection on a changed America." –Chicago Tribune. [2M, 1W, 1 boy] ISBN: 978-0-8222-3183-7

★ **THE HEIR APPARENT by David Ives, adapted from Le Légataire Universel by Jean-François Regnard.** Paris, 1708. Eraste, a worthy though penniless young man, is in love with the fair Isabelle, but her forbidding mother, Madame Argante, will only let the two marry if Eraste can show he will inherit the estate of his rich but miserly Uncle Geronte. Unfortunately, old Geronte has also fallen for the fair Isabelle, and plans to marry her this very day and leave her everything in his will—separating the two young lovers forever. Eraste's wily servant Crispin jumps in, getting a couple of meddling relatives disinherited by impersonating them (one, a brash American, the other a French female country cousin)—only to have the old man kick off before his will is made! In a brilliant stroke, Crispin then impersonates the old man, dictating a will favorable to his master (and Crispin himself, of course)—only to find that rich Uncle Geronte isn't dead at all and is more than ever ready to marry Isabelle! The multiple strands of the plot are unraveled to great comic effect in the streaming rhyming couplets of French classical comedy, and everyone lives happily, and richly, ever after. [4M, 3W] ISBN: 978-0-8222-2808-0

★ **HANDLE WITH CARE by Jason Odell Williams.** Circumstances both hilarious and tragic bring together a young Israeli woman, who has little command of English, and a young American man, who has little command of romance. Is their inevitable love an accident…or is it destiny, generations in the making? "A hilarious and heartwarming romantic comedy." –NY Times. "Hilariously funny! Utterly charming, fearlessly adorable and a tiny bit magical." –Naples News. [2M, 2W] ISBN: 978-0-8222-3138-7

★ **LAST GAS by John Cariani.** Nat Paradis is a Red Sox-loving part-time dad who manages Paradis' Last Convenient Store, the last convenient place to get gas—or anything—before the Canadian border to the north and the North Maine Woods to the west. When an old flame returns to town, Nat gets a chance to rekindle a romance he gave up on years ago. But sparks fly as he's forced to choose between new love and old. "Peppered with poignant characters [and] sharp writing." –Portland Phoenix. "Very funny and surprisingly thought-provoking." –Portland Press Herald. [4M, 3W] ISBN: 978-0-8222-3232-2

DRAMATISTS PLAY SERVICE, INC.
440 Park Avenue South, New York, NY 10016 212-683-8960 Fax 212-213-1539
postmaster@dramatists.com www.dramatists.com

NEW PLAYS

★ **ACT ONE by James Lapine.** Growing up in an impoverished Bronx family and forced to drop out of school at age thirteen, Moss Hart dreamed of joining the glamorous world of the theater. Hart's famous memoir *Act One* plots his unlikely collaboration with the legendary playwright George S. Kaufman and his arrival on Broadway. Tony Award-winning writer and director James Lapine has adapted Act One for the stage, creating a funny, heartbreaking and suspenseful celebration of a playwright and his work. "…brims contagiously with the ineffable, irrational and irrefutable passion for that endangered religion called the Theater." –NY Times. "…wrought with abundant skill and empathy." –Time Out. [8M, 4W] ISBN: 978-0-8222-3217-9

★ **THE VEIL by Conor McPherson.** May 1822, rural Ireland. The defrocked Reverend Berkeley arrives at the crumbling former glory of Mount Prospect House to accompany a young woman to England. Seventeen-year-old Hannah is to be married off to a marquis in order to resolve the debts of her mother's estate. However, compelled by the strange voices that haunt his beautiful young charge and a fascination with the psychic current that pervades the house, Berkeley proposes a séance, the consequences of which are catastrophic. "…an effective mixture of dark comedy and suspense." –Telegraph (London). "A cracking fireside tale of haunting and decay." –Times (London). [3M, 5W] ISBN: 978-0-8222-3313-8

★ **AN OCTOROON by Branden Jacobs-Jenkins. Winner of the 2014 OBIE Award for Best New American Play.** Judge Peyton is dead and his plantation Terrebonne is in financial ruins. Peyton's handsome nephew George arrives as heir apparent and quickly falls in love with Zoe, a beautiful octoroon. But the evil overseer M'Closky has other plans—for both Terrebonne and Zoe. In 1859, a famous Irishman wrote this play about slavery in America. Now an American tries to write his own. "AN OCTOROON invites us to laugh loudly and easily at how naïve the old stereotypes now seem, until nothing seems funny at all." –NY Times [10M, 5W] ISBN: 978-0-8222-3226-1

★ **IVANOV translated and adapted by Curt Columbus.** In this fascinating early work by Anton Chekhov, we see the union of humor and pathos that would become his trademark. A restless man, Nicholai Ivanov struggles to dig himself out of debt and out of provincial boredom. When the local doctor, Lvov, informs Ivanov that his wife Anna is dying and accuses him of worsening her condition with his foul moods, Ivanov is sent into a downward spiral of depression and ennui. He soon finds himself drawn to a beautiful young woman, Sasha, full of hope and energy. Finding himself stuck between a romantic young mistress and his ailing wife, Ivanov falls deeper into crisis, heading toward inevitable tragedy. [8M, 8W] ISBN: 978-0-8222-3155-4

DRAMATISTS PLAY SERVICE, INC.
440 Park Avenue South, New York, NY 10016 212-683-8960 Fax 212-213-1539
postmaster@dramatists.com www.dramatists.com

NEW PLAYS

★ **I'LL EAT YOU LAST: A CHAT WITH SUE MENGERS by John Logan.** For more than 20 years, Sue Mengers' clients were the biggest names in show business: Barbra Streisand, Faye Dunaway, Burt Reynolds, Ali MacGraw, Gene Hackman, Cher, Candice Bergen, Ryan O'Neal, Nick Nolte, Mike Nichols, Gore Vidal, Bob Fosse…If her clients were the talk of the town, she was the town, and her dinner parties were the envy of Hollywood. Now, you're invited into her glamorous Beverly Hills home for an evening of dish, dirty secrets and all the inside showbiz details only Sue can tell you. "A delectable soufflé of a solo show…thanks to the buoyant, witty writing of Mr. Logan" –NY Times. "80 irresistible minutes of primo tinseltown dish from a certified master chef." –Hollywood Reporter. [1W] ISBN: 978-0-8222-3079-3

★ **PUNK ROCK by Simon Stephens.** In a private school outside of Manchester, England, a group of highly-articulate seventeen-year-olds flirt and posture their way through the day while preparing for their A-Level mock exams. With hormones raging and minimal adult supervision, the students must prepare for their future — and survive the savagery of high school. Inspired by playwright Simon Stephens' own experiences as a teacher, PUNK ROCK is an honest and unnerving chronicle of contemporary adolescence. "[A] tender, ferocious and frightning play." –NY Times. "[A] muscular little play that starts out funny and ferocious then reveals its compassion by degrees." –Hollywood Reporter. [5M, 3W] ISBN: 978-0-8222-3288-9

★ **THE COUNTRY HOUSE by Donald Margulies.** A brood of famous and longing-to-be-famous creative artists have gathered at their summer home during the Williamstown Theatre Festival. When the weekend takes an unexpected turn, everyone is forced to improvise, inciting a series of simmering jealousies, romantic outbursts, and passionate soul-searching. Both witty and compelling, THE COUNTRY HOUSE provides a piercing look at a family of performers coming to terms with the roles they play in each other's lives. "A valentine to the artists of the stage." –NY Times. "Remarkably candid and funny." –Variety. [3M, 3W] ISBN: 978-0-8222-3274-2

★ **OUR LADY OF KIBEHO by Katori Hall.** Based on real events, OUR LADY OF KIBEHO is an exploration of faith, doubt, and the power and consequences of both. In 1981, a village girl in Rwanda claims to see the Virgin Mary. Ostracized by her schoolmates and labeled disturbed, everyone refuses to believe, until impossible happenings appear again and again. Skepticism gives way to fear, and then to belief, causing upheaval in the school community and beyond. "Transfixing." –NY Times. "Hall's passionate play renews belief in what theater can do." –Time Out [7M, 8W, 1 boy] ISBN: 978-0-8222-3301-5

DRAMATISTS PLAY SERVICE, INC.
440 Park Avenue South, New York, NY 10016 212-683-8960 Fax 212-213-1539
postmaster@dramatists.com www.dramatists.com

NEW PLAYS

★ **AGES OF THE MOON by Sam Shepard.** Byron and Ames are old friends, reunited by mutual desperation. Over bourbon on ice, they sit, reflect and bicker until fifty years of love, friendship and rivalry are put to the test at the barrel of a gun. "A poignant and honest continuation of themes that have always been present in the work of one of this country's most important dramatists, here reconsidered in the light and shadow of time passed." –NY Times. "Finely wrought…as enjoyable and enlightening as a night spent stargazing." –Talkin' Broadway. [2M] ISBN: 978-0-8222-2462-4

★ **ALL THE WAY by Robert Schenkkan. Winner of the 2014 Tony Award for Best Play.** November, 1963. An assassin's bullet catapults Lyndon Baines Johnson into the presidency. A Shakespearean figure of towering ambition and appetite, this charismatic, conflicted Texan hurls himself into the passage of the Civil Rights Act—a tinderbox issue emblematic of a divided America—even as he campaigns for re-election in his own right, and the recognition he so desperately wants. In Pulitzer Prize and Tony Award–winning Robert Schenkkan's vivid dramatization of LBJ's first year in office, means versus ends plays out on the precipice of modern America. ALL THE WAY is a searing, enthralling exploration of the morality of power. It's not personal, it's just politics. "…action-packed, thoroughly gripping… jaw-dropping political drama." –Variety. "A theatrical coup…nonstop action. The suspense of a first-class thriller." –NY1. [17M, 3W] ISBN: 978-0-8222-3181-3

★ **CHOIR BOY by Tarell Alvin McCraney.** The Charles R. Drew Prep School for Boys is dedicated to the creation of strong, ethical black men. Pharus wants nothing more than to take his rightful place as leader of the school's legendary gospel choir. Can he find his way inside the hallowed halls of this institution if he sings in his own key? "[An] affecting and honest portrait…of a gay youth tentatively beginning to find the courage to let the truth about himself become known." –NY Times. "In his stirring and stylishly told drama, Tarell Alvin McCraney cannily explores race and sexuality and the graces and gravity of history." –NY Daily News. [7M] ISBN: 978-0-8222-3116-5

★ **THE ELECTRIC BABY by Stefanie Zadravec.** When Helen causes a car accident that kills a young man, a group of fractured souls cross paths and connect around a mysterious dying baby who glows like the moon. Folk tales and folklore weave throughout this magical story of sad endings, strange beginnings and the unlikely people that get you from one place to the next. "The imperceptible magic that pervades human existence and the power of myth to assuage sorrow are invoked by the playwright as she entwines the lives of strangers in THE ELECTRIC BABY, a touching drama." –NY Times. "As dazzling as the dialogue is dreamful." –Pittsburgh City Paper. [3M, 3W] ISBN: 978-0-8222-3011-3

DRAMATISTS PLAY SERVICE, INC.
440 Park Avenue South, New York, NY 10016 212-683-8960 Fax 212-213-1539
postmaster@dramatists.com www.dramatists.com